WORLD OF THE
POLAR BEAR
FRED BRUEMMER

WORLD OF THE
POLAR BEAR
FRED BRUEMMER

NorthWord
PRESS, INC

Originally published in Canada by
Key Porter Books, Toronto

Published in The United States by:
NorthWord Press, Inc.
Box 1360
Minocqua, WI 54548

For a free catalog of NorthWord's
line of nature books, tapes and
gifts call 1-800-336-5666.

ISBN 1-55971-036-5

Printed and bound in Italy

89 90 91 92 93 6 5 4 3 2 1

Page one: Two polar bears meet on the ice in the morning.

Page two: A bear family patrols the coast of Hudson Bay.

Page four: A totally relaxed bear.

CONTENTS

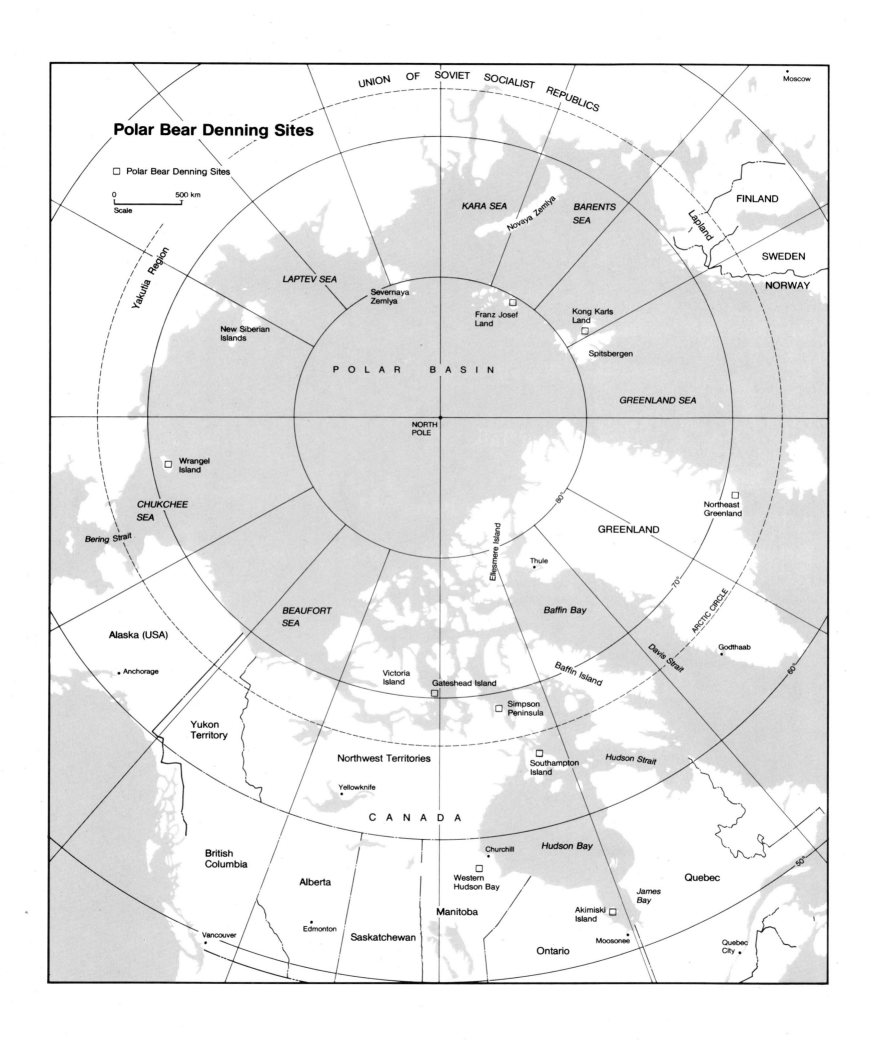

Polar Bear Denning Sites

☐ Polar Bear Denning Sites

0   500 km
Scale

UNION OF SOVIET SOCIALIST REPUBLICS

Moscow

FINLAND

Lapland

SWEDEN

NORWAY

KARA SEA

Novaya Zemlya

BARENTS SEA

Severnaya Zemlya

Franz Josef Land

Kong Karls Land

Spitsbergen

LAPTEV SEA

New Siberian Islands

Yakutia Region

POLAR BASIN

GREENLAND SEA

NORTH POLE

Wrangel Island

80°

Northeast Greenland

CHUKCHEE SEA

Bering Strait

Ellesmere Island

GREENLAND

Thule

70°

ARCTIC CIRCLE

Baffin Bay

BEAUFORT SEA

Davis Strait

Godthaab

60°

Alaska (USA)

Anchorage

Victoria Island

Gateshead Island

Baffin Island

Simpson Peninsula

Yukon Territory

Northwest Territories

Yellowknife

Southampton Island

Hudson Strait

CANADA

British Columbia

Alberta

Churchill

Hudson Bay

Quebec

50°

Western Hudson Bay

James Bay

Manitoba

Saskatchewan

Edmonton

Akimiski Island

Ontario

Quebec City

Vancouver

Moosonee

For Dr. Albert J. Guerraty who gave me a new heart and a new life, so I can return again to the north I love.

And to all the members of the heart transplant team of the Royal Victoria Hospital in Montreal, especially Dr. Derek Marpole, Dr. David H. Fitchett, Dr. J. Novick, Dr. J. Symes, Simone Sirois and Carole Magnan.

To Dr. Magdi H. Sami I am infinitely grateful; when I needed it most, he gave me courage and hope.

And with all my love for Maud, Aurel and René who are a wonderful reason for living.

After swimming across a bay, a mother and her cubs walk on an ice ridge near the sea.

PREFACE

The 1961 Scottish Spitsbergen Expedition man-hauled, in classic British fashion, its heavy sled across the ice cap of Vest Spitsbergen. It was beautiful but desolate. Days passed and we saw no sign of life except an ethereally beautiful, pure white ivory gull, which followed us in hopes of food scraps. We planned to climb Newtontoppen, the highest mountain of the archipelago, an ice-clad cone in a land of ice. When we reached its base, we saw the great tracks of a polar bear in the midst of this infinite solitude.

Since then, polar bears and polar bear people have formed a large part of my life: Inuit who hunted polar bears; scientists who studied them; obsessives like myself who returned year after year to Canada's Cape Churchill to watch the bears, until the bears were no longer just bears, but old acquaintances with names and known and predictable habits.

I am grateful to Akpaleeapik and Akeeagok of Grise Fiord on Ellesmere Island for taking me along on their last great polar bear hunt, before such hunts became history. Inuterssuaq of Greenland's Polar Inuit taught me with great patience the polar bear lore of his people. Jacob Ahkinga of Little Diomede Island in the Bering Strait between Alaska and Siberia told me stories far into the night about bears that travel between the continents.

Dr. Charles Jonkel, then with the Canadian Wildlife Service and now with the University of Montana, let me share in his early studies of polar bears in the 1960s. Dr. Thor Larsen, Norway's great polar bear specialist, told me about the bears and his work in the Svalbard region. Dr. Ian Stirling of the Canadian Wildlife Service, Canada's foremost expert on polar bears, has for 20 years generously shared his immense knowledge with me, and Dennis Andriashek, his long-time assistant, has been equally generous. Dr. Malcolm A. Ramsay studied the polar bears of western Hudson Bay for many years and he has helped me to understand this unique population. In the two summers I spent at the high Arctic camp of Dr. Thomas G. Smith of the Arctic Biological Station, Department of Fisheries and Oceans, I profited greatly from his vast and varied knowledge of the north.

I spent two seasons in a tiny hut atop the tower at Cape Churchill with John Kroeger of New York State, and a better friend and companion one could not have. Dan Guravich, the famous photographer, and I have spent many seasons together at the cape; it is a friendship I greatly cherish. I hope Len Smith of Tundra Buggy Tours Ltd., Churchill, Manitoba, and Roy Bukowsky of Winnipeg, Manitoba, know how much I have enjoyed my trips with them.

Some of my high Arctic trips have been assisted by Canada's Polar Continental Shelf Project and for this I am grateful. My special thanks go to its director, Dr. George Hobson, and to its base managers, Eddie Chapman and Barry Haugh.

A GATHERING
OF BEARS

Every fall polar bears gather at Cape Churchill on the west coast of Hudson Bay. I once saw 45 bears at the cape; others have seen as many as 60. Aerial surveys carried out by the polar bear biologist Ian Stirling of the Canadian Wildlife Service indicate that in October between 600 and 1,000 bears mass along the 100-mile coastal stretch between the Nelson River to the south of the cape and the Churchill River to the north of it. It is the largest concentration of polar bears in the world.

I spent seven seasons at Cape Churchill, two in a tiny cabin atop a 45-foot tower and five in Tundra Buggies designed by Len Smith of Churchill, huge metal-sheathed vehicles, part bus part bunkhouse, which crawl across the rock-strewn terrain on enormous, lightly inflated tires. At first the bears were simply bears, magnificent animals, the young sleekly elegant, the fully mature males awesome in their controlled power. As I watched them for days and weeks, bears became individuals, recognizable by distinctive scars and marks and by personal quirks and manners which changed little with the passing of years. I began to realize bears use signs and signals that mean something to other bears—a warning, a reassurance, an invitation to play—and that they adopt positions and attitudes to which other bears respond in predictable ways.

The bears are creatures of a different realm, yet it is not entirely closed to us. As I watched their rituals, their codes of behavior in the presence of other bears, I felt a tingle of excitement whenever I correctly anticipated action and reaction, the sort of thrill one experiences when one grasps the first words, the first sentences of an unknown language. However, these were mere generalizations; behavior varied greatly from bear to bear and I quickly learned that the animals were highly individualistic. Not only did bears have idiosyncrasies that modified general behavior, but their behavior also changed with age and social standing.

I saw bears rise in the hierarchy of bears from fearful, insecure striplings to supreme males, relaxed and regal in the realization of their indisputed power. Others, inevitably, declined. One great male was past his prime when I first met him at the cape, yet still powerful enough to command the respect of other bears. But year after year his body aged, his status diminished, his temper changed. He became a bitter old bear, cantankerous and suspicious, dangerous, unpredictable and quick to take offence, who lunged in vicious, fearful anger at

Left: A gathering of bears. As many as 60 bears have been seen together at Cape Churchill, Manitoba.

Above: A curious young bear watches another bear approach.

younger, more powerful bears that passed. The last time I met him, I only recognized him because of a distinctive chevron-shaped scar that zigzagged down the side of his neck. He was dreadfully emaciated, the skin stretched tautly over the curved, protruding spine. His once big belly had shrunk and his legs seemed abnormally long and lanky.

Polar bears are usually fastidiously clean; they lick their paws after every meal and rub and roll in dry snow to remove all fat and blood from their fur. His fur was filthy, brown and matted. His eyes were bleary and bloodshot. He walked slowly, with a painful, arthritic stiffness and once he lay down appeared to have trouble getting up. His attitude now was one of nearly constant fear and hostility. He was such a time-ravaged monarch that, in pity, Anne Fadiman of LIFE magazine, who shared that fall with me at the cape, called him King Lear.

Some bears were obsessed with *idées fixes*, usually centered, as most of the polar bears' ideas seem to be, upon the procurement of food. It was one huge male's firm conviction that if he shook our tower hard enough and long enough, we would fall off. He did it the first year we lived on the tower and he did it again the following year. He shook the tower every time he visited us and he also shook other observation towers along the Hudson Bay coast. A few other bears did it, too, but half-heartedly and, since it procured no food, soon gave up. If, however, attempts to shake biologists and photographers off observation towers had produced frequent and gratifying results, it might have become an adopted habit of the bears of this area, for polar bears are opportunistic, learn quickly and develop regional specialties.

Long ago, the polar bears of Labrador caught salmon in a manner identical to that employed by Alaska's Kodiak bears and the brown bears of Siberia. When the explorer John Cabot sailed along the Labrador coast in 1498, he saw "great plentie of beares in those regions, which use to eate fysshe. For plungeing theym selves into the water where they perceve a multitude of these fysshes to lye, they fasten their clawes in their scales, and so drawe them to lande and eate them." The Labrador polar bears have vanished. Warming weather in the 19th century and the use of firearms by natives and European settlers first diminished and then destroyed this population. With them ended salmon and char fishing by polar bears, for it seems to have been a specialty known only to the Labrador bears.

It has long been assumed that polar bears are loners that roam the vastness of the north, solitary and sour-tempered. Male polar bears, said the explorer-writer Peter Freuchen, are among "the loneliest creatures on Earth . . . [they always] keep some distance apart and never approach each other." Thor Larsen, Norway's foremost polar bear specialist, agrees: "When bears occasionally meet on the ice or on the tundra," he says, "they will pass each other at distances of fifty to one hundred meters or more." This may be the rule, but at Cape Churchill, where these powerful individualists do meet and congregate, they

Male polar bears are among "the loneliest creatures on Earth . . . [they always] keep some distance apart and never approach each other."

—Peter Freuchen, Danish explorer-writer

"After his meal, like all proper bears, he cleaned his fur, head and paws with snow."

—Dr. Erik S. Nyholm, Finnish ethologist, who spent two years (1968–69 and 1971–72) with polar bears on Svalbard

maintain peace and even amity by observing a complex set of rules and rituals. Theirs is a hierarchy where everyone knows, or should know, his place.

At the bottom of the hierarchy are the youngest bears, recently abandoned by their mothers, some three years old, others not yet two. Then in ascending order by size, age, condition and weight come the other bears, to the pinnacle of prestige held by the most powerful males, fat, glossy-furred, muscle-packed individuals that may weigh a thousand pounds or more. As a rule, the powerful treat the weaker with indifferent tolerance, and the weak are meek and cautiously respectful near the big bears. Most unpredictable of all bears are the young and the very old. The young may not as yet have learned proper bear manners; the old are perhaps too touchy and grouchy to care. Both are often famished; they are insecure and fearful and that makes them aggressive. One day a small bear, desperately hungry, rushed at a bear five times his weight and snatched his food away. It was such an incredible breach of bear decorum, the great bear just stood there and glowered. (He may also have known that pursuit was useless because scared little bears can run faster than big fat males.)

To live among bears is strangely fascinating. They seem a part of us; one feels a sense of identification, an odd attraction, vague shadows from our remotest past when, as ancient fables tell, man and bear were really one. Studies carried out by the zoologist Desmond Morris show that the polar bear is one of the world's ten "most popular" animals.

Two bears sleep near the tower when the naturalist John Kroeger and I arrive for our second visit at Cape Churchill. They hear the helicopter and rush away in a frightened, porcine gallop. More than 1,000 bears have been tranquilized and tagged in the Churchill region. They associate the helicopter with fear and pain, flee the moment they hear its distinctive sound and often try to hide in willow thickets or among uptilted ice floes and pressure ridges. The grinding, growling noise of the huge Tundra Buggies does not scare the bears. It often attracts those familiar with the machines. They nonchalantly amble up, lean against the side of the vehicle and try to mooch food from the inmates.

A broad pebble-covered esker meanders across Cape Churchill from east to west, the sediment of a sub-glacial river from the last Ice Age. Two miles to the east of the tower, the cape ends in a crescentic, boulder-strewn spur that hooks out into the dark waters of Hudson Bay. To the south are marshy tundra ponds, hemmed by willow thickets. To the north is the shallow La Pérouse Bay, already frozen, named after the French captain and explorer Jean-François de Galaup, comte de La Pérouse, who raided this bleak coast in 1782.

To Europeans the allure of the north consisted (and still consists) of minerals and furs. The "principall wealth" of Lapland, the Norse chief Othere told King Alfred the Great of England in 890 A.D., consisted of the "skinnes of wild beastes, . . . feathers of birds, . . . whale bones [baleen] . . . and tacklings for shippes made of horse-whale [walrus] and seales skinnes . . ." George Best, chronicler of Sir Martin Frobisher's 1578 expedition to Baffin Island, noted that "I finde in all the Countrie nothing, that may be to delite in, either of pleasure or of accompte, only the shewe of Mine, both of golde, siluer, yron and black lead." (Nearly 400 years later, in the 1960s, the senior executive of a Canadian mining company said about the Arctic: "We're not really all that interested in the scenery and the animals. What we want to do is to make some money out of it.")

To safeguard its control of Hudson Bay and the immense fur wealth of the hinterland, the British Hudson's Bay Company built Prince of Wales's Fort upon the tundra just north of the Churchill River. The second largest stone fortress in North America—its walls 40 feet thick, its embrasures bristling with 42 cannons so large it took ten men to fire one—was a wonder and a marvel to the Indians and the Inuit of the region. When the waves of Europe's wars lapped against the far shores of Hudson Bay, the British were poorly prepared. Only 39 men were at the fort and its commander, the veteran explorer and trader Samuel Hearne, surrendered it without a fight to the French fleet under La Pérouse. Hearne, taken as prisoner to France, returned to Churchill in 1783 to resume trading and to compile meticulous notes about the animals of the Hudson Bay coast, including the polar bears which were then "very common in this region."

While we haul our provisions up to the hut on the tower, a polar bear, reassured by the departure of the helicopter, ambles towards us. He walks slowly, ponderously. Because of the polar bear's rolling, pigeon-toed gait, 19th-century whalers called him the "farmer." He stops, raises his elegant triangular head; sniffs, weaving slightly from side to side; then shuffles on. He is a young male, high-rumped and low-shouldered, his long fur yellowish in the soft evening light. He seems neither afraid nor aggressive, just intensely curious.

The polar bears assemble near Cape Churchill in fall and early winter to wait for ice to form on Hudson Bay. In winter, spring and early summer they hunt upon the ice of the seal-rich sea. Recent aerial surveys carried out by Thomas G. Smith of Canada's Arctic Biological Station show that Hudson Bay is home to about half a million ringed seals, the polar bear's principal prey.

In July, the prevailing northerly winds drive the disintegrating ice, and the bears, towards the southwest coast of Hudson Bay. Marooned on shore, the polar bears, the largest land carnivores on earth, eat anything available: grasses, sedges, seaweed, carrion, berries. They raid eider colonies and eat the eggs. Eight-hundred-pound bears have been seen hunting two-ounce lemmings. A few bears wander south as far as Moosonee at the head of James Bay, nearly on the latitude of London, England. Many just sleep, often in shallow pits scooped out on sandy ridges near the sea, living off the fat reserves accumulated during the bountiful hunts of winter and spring.

The Hudson's Bay Company surveyor-explorer Peter Fidler rounded Cape

The polar bear "is a noble-looking animal and of enormous strength, living bravely and warm amid eternal ice . . . They are the unrivaled master-existences of this icebound solitude."

—John Muir, American naturalist in northern Alaska, 1881

Wave-sculptured ice on a high Arctic coast.

Churchill by canoe on August 22, 1807, and "saw 5 White Bears upon" the tiny islet near the tip of the cape. In fall the bears amble northward and bunch at this and other capes, impatiently awaiting the freeze-up that will end their long summer fast and enable them to catch fat seals again upon the ice of Hudson Bay.

By the time we have hauled up and stowed provisions and water for three weeks, 14 bears are in the vicinity of the tower. Moist snow falls softly, evenly. Great peace and quiet fill the land. The bears have no fear of us but wander about with that innocent air of animals in a Breughel painting of paradise. This is Indian country. Indians were a people of the land. They hunted and ate black bears but feared and avoided the much larger, ghostly-white bears of the coast and the ice. The bears had no enemies, no one to fear. There were no humans (except a few anchorite Irish monks) on Iceland before the Vikings discovered and settled it in the 9th century and, records *Egil's Saga*, ". . . all creatures were at their ease . . . for men were unknown to them."

The light is fading; snow gently blurs landscape and bears as in a pointillistic painting. I climb down the tower and perch on the 12-foot rung above the ground. A bear comes to investigate. He rears up directly beneath me, leans with his huge, sharp-clawed, fur-fringed paws against the tower for support and looks earnestly at me with small, deep-brown, slightly slanted eyes. We are only inches apart but, unless I slip and fall, I am quite safe. The bear is already on tiptoe and cannot reach higher. His large, black, minutely pitted nose twitches. He lives in a world of smells. His sense of smell is more than 100 times better than mine; he can smell a dead whale 15 miles away or a ringed seal pup in its *nunarjak*, its birth lair, through three to six feet of compacted arctic snow. What sort of mental image does my smell evoke in his mind?

I talk softly to the bear. He keeps sniffing, then yawns deeply, showing his great ivory-yellow teeth and the purplish lining of his mouth. When two bears meet, ostentatious yawning is a signal of appeasement, a sign of peace. Does this bear try to tell me in his body language that he means no harm, that he is friendly and very curious? He obviously trusts me. But do I trust him? The temptation to touch him is very great.

Long ago I did pet a polar bear. The thrill of that moment is still with me, although I now realize it was a foolish thing to do. She was Linda, a very gentle four-year-old bear we had caught in a steel-cable snare not far from Churchill. We kept her captive while waiting for a radio collar to arrive that, we hoped, would enable us to track Linda in her future wanderings. I visited her every day and fed her strips of fat and meat I bought from the Hudson's Bay Company butcher in Churchill. She picked them up carefully and soon was obviously looking forward to my visits. Then, yielding to temptation, I fed her by hand and she took the food cautiously from my fingers. She could easily have snapped, held and killed me, for polar bears, despite their bulky appearance, can move with lightning speed. But she never tried. And finally I touched her. She watched the approaching hand with slightly lowered head, the hair on neck and back abristle, a sign of latent apprehension and fear. But she did not growl or hiss or threaten. The hair upon her head was short and silky soft. She ducked a bit as I touched her and then remained quiet as I gently stroked her head. I was filled with excitement and elation; adrenalin, no doubt, but also something else—the thrill, however brief and tenuous, of a shared bond and trust.

Now I am older, perhaps wiser, certainly more cautious. I only talk to bears. I do not touch them anymore. The bear beneath me keeps sniffing; his head moves slightly from side to side. I stare into his eyes and nearly immediately he becomes uneasy. To stare is aggressive and in bear society it is impolite and impolitic. He looks away, shifts position; there is suddenly a sense of tension. He drops to the ground and walks away.

"We see, we talk, and we dream more of bears than of any other animals, . . ."

—Sir F. Leopold M'Clintock, RN., who spent two years (1857–59) in the Canadian high Arctic searching for the lost Franklin expedition

Scientists study polar bear behavior from a 45-foot high tower at Cape Churchill.

Above: A female king eider, left, followed by her courting drake on a lake in the high Arctic.

Left: The last rays of the setting sun catch a polar bear patrolling an arctic coast.

Left: An undecided or embarrassed bear often rubs his paws in a vague and worried fashion.

Above: A scarred old warrior. Bears are amiable during fall encounters, but rival males fight furiously during the mating season.

Opposite: In Churchill, the "Polar Bear Capital of the World," the bears are a major tourist attraction. Visitors see the bears from the safety of Tundra Buggies.

Above: Winter near Churchill. Polar bears gather in this region before heading out onto the new-formed ice of Hudson Bay.

Top left: A young male, about four years old, walks on the ice near shore.

Bottom left: The setting sun outlines the elegant head of a polar bear.

BEAR TALK

The smell of sizzling breakfast bacon rouses bears two miles away. They lie blanketed by the snow that fell all night. Now, as the enticing odor wafts towards the cape and we watch with binoculars, snow-covered heads pop up, dark noses twitch and test, bears rise like mounds of snow come to life, shake clouds of snow out of their fur and amble towards the tower. The bears near the tower are all young males, four to six years old, weighing between 250 and 600 pounds. They already know one another and are casually relaxed. But newcomers worry them. Initial encounters between bears tend to be formal, ritualized and tinged with mutual apprehension.

Two bears circle and sniff, walking very slowly. They look slightly past each other, mouths closed, lower lips thrust out like amiable Hapsburgs, signaling peaceful intent and mutual respect by subtle body movements, presumably evaluating by smell and sight each other's size, power, temper and hierarchical standing. They halt and face each other, then approach in slow motion, the smaller bear, low and submissive, taking the initiative. They sniff, dark noses touching. Jaws agape, they mouth each other, then chew gently at each other's necks like horses that groom one another.

The introduction has been made. They have "told" each other by mutually intelligible signs that they are friendly bears. Henceforth they are relaxed in each other's presence. They may ignore each other. Or they may strike up a friendship that can last for the days or weeks they spend together at the cape.

Considering that these animals are powerful enough to kill a 600-pound bearded seal with one stroke of the paw, or crush its skull with one bite, they are amazingly cautious and gentle with one another. The explorer Vilhjalmur Stefansson, who had many encounters with bears, concluded that "with all their strength and splendid weapons of teeth and claws, they are generally retiring." Life is not always that amiable in polar bear society. Most adult males carry large, jagged scars on head, neck, shoulders and rump, mementos of vicious fights among rival males during the mating season in spring. But now at the cape, fights could lead to injury, would waste precious energy and bring no gain in food or sex, so the pragmatic bears avoid them. A few bears become friends. Some play together for hours. Special friends even eat together, share the same snow pit and sleep entwined, like lovers. Most bears simply ignore one another; they are polite but distant. The general atmosphere among the bears at the cape is one of benign neutrality.

Left: Two bears in late summer on an ice-polished, lichen-encrusted rock ridge.

Above: The opening moves of a play-fight are as gentle and stylized as a minuet.

Towards noon a giant bear arrives. We recognize him instantly: it is the tower shaker, the largest, leanest, meanest bear I've ever met, known to various biologists as Nasty, Beelzebub or BOB (an acronym for Bag of Bones). We call him Cassius; he has that lean and hungry look, and we immediately move up to the 18-foot above the ground rung, for last year Cassius nearly got John. In a drastic departure from what we by then had come to regard as proper bear behavior, he marched straight to the tower, reared up and in one swift smooth motion tried to hook John off his perch. It was so sudden, so unexpected, it nearly succeeded. He was also much larger than any of the other bears and could reach 14 feet up. His claws caught John just below the knee but slipped on the smooth, high-quality windproof pants, and before the bear could try again, John swung one rung higher. For a moment the great bear seemed baffled and then he began to rock the tower rhythmically, building momentum with each enormously powerful push. The whole huge metal structure (strong enough to withstand 100 mph winds) began to sway and rattle, the steel guys alternately going slack and tautening with a crack. He kept that up for several minutes and then he sat, chewed on one of the girders, though not hard enough to injure his teeth, while frothy saliva oozed from his mouth, and stared at us with a certain yearning.

This year Cassius repeats in every detail what he did the year before. It is a strange sensation, like watching the replay of a brief segment of one's past. He comes straight to the tower, rears up, tries to reach us, rocks the tower, chews on the girder, then sits and glares at us. The intervening year has been good to him, as it has been to most bears at the cape. The winter was cold and long, the ice thick on Hudson Bay. It broke up three weeks later than usual, seal hunting conditions were probably excellent, the bears gorged on blubber, their favorite food, and many are still swathed in fat. This accounts, in part, for their amiability this year and their willingness to play with one another.

Fat bears are usually friendly and rarely, if ever, attack without serious provocation. In Alaska, noted the American anthropologist Richard Nelson, polar bears "are generally quite timid. Whether they see a man from a distance or are suddenly confronted, they nearly always run away. Well-fed bears are particularly unlikely to bother with man . . ." The Polar Inuit of northwest Greenland left old women alone in summer on islands and on shore, to dry meat and fish and to guard meat caches, certain that no bear would come along and eat meat, fish and guardian, because, said Peter Freuchen, ". . . during the summer [when they are fat] no bear would attack a human being."

At Cape Churchill, hungry bears are nervous and irritable. Driven by hunger, their behavior is erratic and unpredictable. These are often young bears, still inexperienced hunters, and old bears whose hunting prowess is declining. Such bears can be dangerous. "It is only when wounded or pressed by extreme hunger that the polar bear becomes fierce . . ." said the English explorer Sir F. Leopold M'Clintock who spent the years 1857 to 1859 in Canada's high Arctic

The bears' "unwary approach [to people] . . . must not be set down as lack of intelligence. They simply have not the data upon which to reason, for they never before have encountered any dangerous animal upon the ice."

—Vilhjalmur Stefansson, Arctic explorer, 1913

searching for traces of the missing Franklin expedition. A bear made desperate and reckless by hunger is a fearsome animal and even a young bear is terrifyingly powerful.

In 1983, two bears attacked people at oil drilling installations in the Beaufort Sea. One hit and killed the foreman of a seismic camp "and loped away easily with the 235-pound body." The other bear climbed aboard a frozen-in crew barge, killed an 18-year-old driller and carried him off "like a dog carries a stick." In the feeble light of dawn, the other men from the barge followed the bear across the ice. They had no gun. They fired flare guns at the bear; the missiles hissed through the air and lit up ice and bear in eerie brilliance. But the bear did not let go of its prey. One of the men recalled: "The bear would stand up and shake the body like a dog with a woodchuck . . . It was terrible to watch a man being eaten." The bears were killed by Royal Canadian Mounted Police officers. Both bears were three years old and both were emaciated from starvation.

Thor Larsen, Norway's polar bear specialist, has ". . . experienced half a dozen attacks from polar bears . . ." but, he adds in fairness, "I must admit that they all have been provoked." The angered bear attacks with speed and determination. "A provoked bear," said Larsen, "will often signal warnings by blowing air through its nose or by smacking its teeth together. The attack comes surprisingly fast. The animal seems very determined. The head is kept low, the bear moves towards the intruder at a surprising speed. Sometimes it attacks in long, cat-like jumps, without uttering a sound, or perhaps groaning. The bear becomes a tremendous concentration of strength and power, and there is little time left for escape."

Cassius who, in his prime, may have weighed 1,200 to 1,500 pounds, weighed barely 800 pounds the previous year, a gaunt and haggard giant with an evil temper. Since then he has gained at least 200 pounds, but his temper has not improved. He is morose, tetchy and unpredictable and threatens or attacks other bears with little provocation and virtually no warning. The other bears fear him and behave in his presence like people stuck in a subway car with a loud, obnoxious and pushy drunk: they avoid eye contact, try to ease away, pretend to be oblivious, and hope he will pick on someone else. The old bear seems without fear. Ian Stirling tries to visit us by helicopter. All bears run away. Only Cassius remains. He stands, head lowered, and stares at the approaching machine. The pilot tilts the helicopter and the rotor noise turns into a deafening, clattering roar. But the gaunt giant of a bear just stands there, motionless, and glowers at the machine, daring it to land. Finally it rises and flies away, and Cassius returns to the pit he has dug into a snowdrift near the tower.

For three days Cassius reigns supreme. Our coterie of bears avoids him. One evening a huge bear arrives from the south and walks leisurely down the esker, immense power in slow motion, thick wads of muscle rippling beneath his immaculate, silver-glistening coat. He is not as long as Cassius, but he is round and sleek and must weigh more than a thousand pounds, a great male at or near his prime. Our entourage of younger males circles him with conspicuous caution and deference. Since his appearance is so regal, we call him Caesar.

He snuffles around the tower, licks the pebbles where we have poured down bacon fat with his long, bluish tongue, then shuffles towards the snowbank where Cassius sleeps. The old bear gets up instantly. The hairs rise on his neck and back. His head held low, he stares at the approaching bear. He puffs out his upper lip and huffs and hisses menacingly like a cornered cat. The newcomer halts, sniffs, hesitates, then inches forward. The gaunt bear champs loudly, rapidly; froth trickles from his muzzle. He seems to become more compact. It is the steely tension that precedes a lightning charge. John and I, cameras ready, expect an epic fight. But nothing happens. The big male does not want to fight; a fight would prove nothing, achieve nothing and both bears might get severely hurt. Caesar stands still, head slightly averted, yawns ostentatiously, thrusts out his lower lip, slowly backs up, then turns and walks away with feigned indifference. Cassius becomes limp and sinks back into his pit. Henceforth the two great bears avoid each other.

After days of moist, mild weather, it becomes intensely cold. The sun rises, a pale-orange disk over a land infinitely still and serene. A faint roseate blush suffuses the air and delicately tints the sea and ice and bears. In this pearly Monet light, a large flock of ptarmigan settles on the willows near the frozen pond and busily snips the buds. They look like bolls of cotton on the bare bushes. Ptarmigan are immensely numerous in this region. The English explorer Sir Thomas Button and his crew, who wintered near the mouth of the Nelson River south of Cape Churchill in 1612–13, killed "1,800 dozen" ptarmigan. They also killed and ate polar bears but those may have been fatal meals. Polar bears are often infested with trichinae. That winter many of Button's men died, probably of trichinosis.

Another flock of ptarmigan arrives and settles near the bushes. The birds run across the snow on large, densely feathered feet. A polar bear who sleeps nearby gets up and wanders over, not really hopeful but idly intrigued. The birds seem to ignore him. His walk becomes a stalk, cautious now, and low, and tense. At 20 feet he charges, an explosion of fantastic force, a blur of yellow across the ground. The ptarmigan cackle in alarm, clatter upward in a parabolic arc and settle on bushes farther away. The bear, resigned, lies down and falls asleep.

The bears eat anything we give them but their favorite food is blubber and sardines. We roast sardines from time to time upon the Coleman stove to attract bears, and the oily-sickly smell of burned sardines permeates our clothing.

Once, on a trip to the cape, an arctic fox came close to the Tundra Buggy. Since no bears were in sight, I climbed down from the vehicle and made friends with the fox. It was intensely cold and still; the frozen snow squealed shrilly with every step. The white fox danced around me, one moment tiny and abject, ears pressed to his head, the long bushy tail tucked against his side and

Polars bears ". . . are of dreadful ferocity. They seem to give a preference to human blood . . ."

—Thomas Pennant, English author of *Arctic Zoology*, published in London in 1784

then, eager for food, he dashed forward to pick up a sardine. After half an hour, he ate from my hand, bit into my sardine-soaked heavy leather glove and tugged and growled when I did not let go.

Suddenly the fox stopped, glanced past me, spun around and raced away. I turned cautiously. Fifteen feet behind me stood a polar bear, a 600-pound male, who was watching me with great interest. He had approached so silently, not even the fox, with hearing so acute he can detect the squeak of little lemmings through two feet of snow, had heard him. I got up slowly. The bear watched, his nose twitching. The faint breeze was from me to him; it must have been laden with delicious smells. Head high, ears erect, mouth closed, eyes averted, the bear signaled "peace," but he was also extremely interested. When I backed up, he followed. At ten feet, I threw him a glove. He grabbed it, bit into it, then put it on the snow, placed one massive, sharp-clawed paw upon it and, with great deliberation, extracted the woolen inner mitten, as one would remove an offending bit of string from a roast beef dinner. Then, without much effort, he tore the glove to pieces and ate it. This gave me time to reach the safety of the Tundra Buggy and, when he followed, I threw him the other glove.

Not all bears are so amiable. William Scoresby, the famous 19th-century English whaler-scientist, moored his ship to a huge ice floe off East Greenland. A large bear was on the floe and a sailor "emboldened by artificial courage derived from rum . . ." took a whale-lance and went up to the bear. The bear advanced, the sailor lost his nerve, threw down his lance and ran. The bear was soon ". . . at the heels of the panting seaman who dropped one of his mittens to distract him . . . then dropped another mitten, then a hat, which the creature tore to shreds between paws and teeth. Now rapidly loosing strength, the adventurer might have met the fate of his garments had not his shipmates sallied to his rescue . . . The Bear came to a standstill, seeming to survey his enemies like an experienced general. Finding them too numerous for hope of success, he very wisely wheeled about in safe and honorable retreat."

Most bears near the tower are politely distant with one another. But when food is involved, rank asserts itself. Large bears take precedence. While Caesar eats our offerings, smaller bears sidle up, hoping for leftovers, but they are lowly and careful and when Caesar growls, they shy away. Prior possession of food, however, does confer some rights in bear society. When smaller bears are first at the food, Caesar approaches slowly, cautiously, but with considerable persistence. The small bears roar and threaten, Caesar stops, then eases forward and, reluctantly, the smaller bears make room for him. Despite Freuchen's assertion that if a young bear tries to defend his food "he is invariably slain by the older bear," the big bears at the cape seem loath to fight even with bears a third their weight. They eat side by side but, among the smaller bears, growling and abristle, there is tension and fear.

Only bears that arrive in pairs share food in harmony. They are either siblings or young males, or males that form friendships during their stay at the

"*Both big bears devoured seal blubber in harmony, and they licked one another's lips and throats as I often saw sister bears do.*"

—Dr. Erik S. Nyholm, Finnish biologist who spent two years (1968–69 and 1971–72) with polar bears on Svalbard

cape. Female bears leave their cubs when they are two or three years old. The cubs, suddenly alone, often travel together, for weeks and sometimes for months. They share meals and find comfort in each other's company. The nicest pair I met were Ozzie and Harriet, named by writer Richard C. Davids and by photographer Dan Guravich, with whom I have spent so many seasons at Cape Churchill.

Brother and sister were nearly three years old and in splendid condition, their fur immaculate. Ozzie was roundish: his ears were round and densely furred; his rump was round; his belly round. He was a fat and friendly bear. Harriet, a third smaller than her brother, was also friendly but shier and more cautious. As a special treat, we gave them a bucketful of rotten blubber. To polar bears, this is ambrosia. They love blubber above all else, regardless of its age. The siblings delicately ate the brownish, semi-liquid, putrid mess and the blubber-soaked snow beneath. When they grabbed a big piece together, they tore it apart without the slightest sign of jealousy or animosity. After the meal they licked their paws and each other's faces, removing all traces of fat.

During the next two weeks, Harriet remained shy and diffident, but Ozzie became the special friend of Len Smith, the designer of the Tundra Buggies. When Len called, Ozzie came, reared up, leaned against the vehicle with his huge fur-fringed paws and looked soulfully at Len. Len talked to him. Ozzie smelled bread, sardines, and other wonderful odors and twitched his large black nose. Len gave him bread and Ozzie took the pieces carefully from his fingers with extended mobile lips. After a few days it was hard to say who was training whom. Ozzie knew Len's voice and came promptly when Len called him. But when Len was resting and Ozzie felt like having a snack, he came to the vehicle and pounded its metal wall with a massive paw. Len promptly got up and fed him bread and sometimes sardines. Len Smith was immensely pleased with his "pet bear." But one had the distinct impression that the bear was also very pleased with Len Smith.

The bear pairs near our tower play a lot this year. The year before the bears were lean and could not afford to waste precious energy on frivolity. Now most bears are sleekly fat and some play-fight for hours. These mock combats look ferocious but they are extremely ritualized and civilized. The bears that play are usually between four and eight years old and weigh 300 to 750 pounds. Males in their prime, great muscle-packed, 1,000-pounders like Caesar, do not play-fight anymore. Young bears, the recently abandoned two- or three-year-olds, rarely play. They are usually hungry and, suddenly motherless among this horde of larger bears, feel intimidated and are not in the mood for play. Very old bears never play. They appear bent, grouchy, and arthritic, well past both play and passion. Only fear or the prospect of food rouses them.

A male near our tower feels like playing. He approaches his friend, another male of nearly equal size, and they begin a slow-motion ursine *pas de deux*. They

"Though such a tremendous animal, they are very shy of coming near a man."

—Samuel Hearne, Hudson's Bay Company trader, Churchill, 1760s

Bears on shorefast ice near Cape Churchill.

circle and sniff, and then approach each other. One places a massive paw upon the other's shoulder, they rise and push and spar, embrace to keep their balance and waltz around and around in the snow. One topples and lies on his back, huge furry paws pedaling in the air. The other, jaws agape, throws himself on top and grabs his chum by the throat. They romp and roll and wrestle in the snow. They pant so loud, we can hear them several hundred feet away. Puffs of hot breath dance in the icy air. Considering their awesome power, the bears practice marvelous restraint and are extremely careful not to hurt each other. They play with immense enjoyment, like two gigantic, shaggy puppies having a romp. Finally, exhausted, they sprawl on the snow and gulp snow to cool their overheated bodies. After a rest of 20 minutes, one bear gets up, nuzzles and nudges his prone friend and, after some prodding, the play-fight begins anew.

These fights are probably a form of training, common among young males of many species, for the fierce fights for dominance in future mating seasons. This may be the proper Darwinian explanation, but watching the wrestling bears for so many years, I feel they do it partly for fun, a bit of high-spirited roughhousing carefully controlled by well-observed rules.

The bears that play together are nearly always of equal size. Occasionally a large bear in the mood for play approaches a little bear, but the invitation is rarely taken up. The large bear advances slowly and lowly, and signals his intentions for peace, friendship and play as explicitly as possible. The little bear, apprehensive and as bristly as a frightened hedgehog, keeps backing up; both wander around the cape, one forward and one backward, until the small bear wheels and flees.

On very rare occasions, the gentleness of the large bear will allay the small bear's fears and they carefully play together. In such unequal play-fights initiated by a large bear, the little bear nearly always "wins." The large one, powerful enough to severely injure his small opponent with one swat, uses utmost caution not to intimidate the little fellow, because that would instantly end the fight and the fun. So he lets himself be pummeled and pushed by the smaller bear and frequently goes limp and collapses. In one bout that I watched between a 700-pound bear and a 300-pound bear, the big bear toppled 11 times, the little bear only once.

Until now, all bears that have come to Cape Churchill have been males. Large hungry males may, on rare occasions, pursue and kill cubs, and they may even kill the mother who will fight to the death for her young. The females therefore avoid the cape and its massed male bears. But as the days get colder and ice fringes the dark water of Hudson Bay, the lure of ice and seals becomes strong and a few mothers and cubs come to the cape.

A female and two two-year-old cubs walk down the esker. One cub, a timid female, walks behind her mother. The brother, nearly as big as his mother but not as heavy, trots ahead. The mother huffs and calls. The young male ignores her. The smells from our tower attract him; the presence of so many bears means there is food. Like all polar bear mothers, the female "talks" frequently to her cubs, admonishes, reproves and calls them to order with abrupt throaty commands. When they are small and disobedient, she may cuff them. But these are teenagers, near independence, the little female still shy and obedient, the male cocksure and adventurous. Our coterie of males ignores the new arrivals; some ease away because few males care to tackle the hair-trigger-tempered mothers with cubs.

The big cub, hungry and brash, muscles in among the adults. He moans to incite his mother and charges a male several times his size. The mother immediately comes to his aid and together they rout the big bear who does not want to fight. The cub uses this ploy again and again. To get at food, he attacks larger bears and when they turn on him, he calls plaintively for his mother who instantly becomes all fury and attacks. Later, when their mother leaves them, such cocky cubs quickly learn meekness and bear manners, for while large males may yield to an angry mother, they can turn in deadly anger upon a lone and uppity youngster. One little male, recently abandoned, yelled frantically for his mother when a provoked large male lunged at him. But there was no mother to protect him and from then on the badly frightened little bear knew just how low he stood in the bear society at Cape Churchill.

A crimson sun sets over a hushed and frozen land. The bears stand upon the esker, massive dark shapes limned in gold. At night the northern lights are spectacular. Constantly changing, streamers and whorls and curtains of greenish-white shift and sway across the sky. They flare and flow in eerie splendor across the velvet black of night, change to deep violet and back to pale green, the silent dance of spectral fire. "Who but God can conceive such infinite scenes of glory," wrote the 19th-century American explorer Charles Francis Hall. To the Norse, the shifting, swaying lights were the Valkyrie racing across the heavens. The Inuit believed they were the souls of the dead at play. Stars glitter through the icy air: Polaris, the North Star, and Arctos, the constellation of the Bear, that gave its name to the Arctic.

Man's fascination with bears is ancient. He has feared them, killed them, worshiped them. The bears that pad so restlessly below me in the dark beneath the glittering stars and the flowing aurora are part of our past, part of the north, part of that vast tapestry of fable and mythology about man and bears that was central to the culture of most circumpolar people, from Lapps to Kets to Ainu and Inuit. Bears may have been man's first gods. People in northern Norway (and most parts of Siberia) reported the 19th-century British traveler James Lamont, were loath to use the word *bear* and used circumlocutions instead, just as to the Hebrews *Yaweh* was the ineffable name of Jehovah. Bears walk with us through time; they are the essence and emblem of the north. The escutcheon of 12th-century Viking Greenland carried a polar bear sejant.

Left: Bears circle, taking each other's measure. If they feel compatible, they will come close, sniff, mouth and play.

Previous pages: Initial encounters are polite but cautious.

Above: In bear society, sniffing is a form of introduction.

Above: The bears rise and embrace.   *Top right:* The ostentatious yawn is a sign of peace and friendship.   *Bottom right:* They wrestle in the snow.

Left: Ritualized mouthing. With jaws agape, the great bears come together but they are careful not to injure each other.

Left: Two bears are still eager to play. A third, too hot, lies prone upon the snow.

Top: Bear on ice: cooling off after a hectic play-fight.

Bottom: A tired bear curls up and goes to sleep.

Overleaf: A polar bear on the gold ice of late evening.

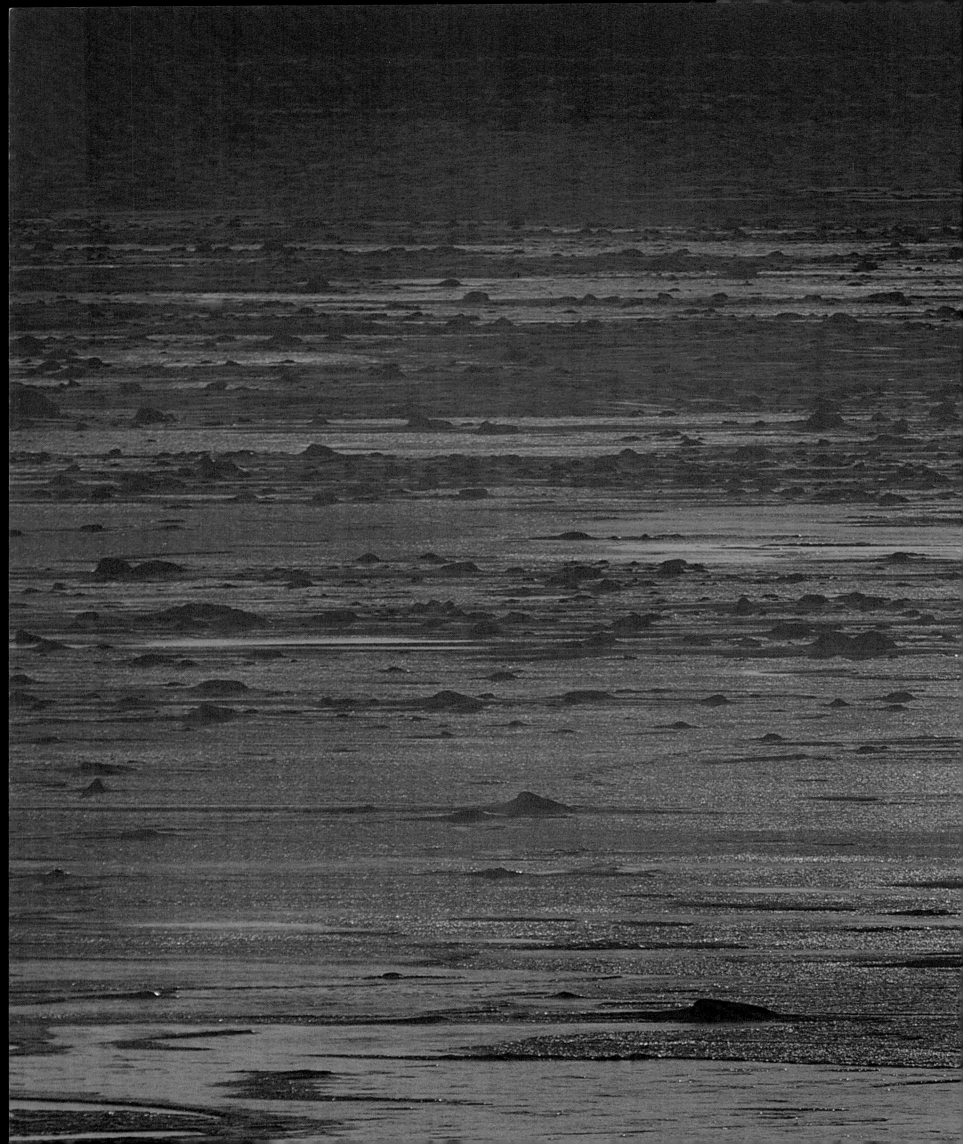

After a dispute over food, a yearling bear chases a young male along the coast.

A brother and a sister bear tear a piece of meat in two.

Above: Lured by food smells, a polar bear takes the highway towards the town of Churchill.

Top left: An oil rig in the Beaufort Sea. To minimize bear problems, all garbage is taken to shore and burned.

Bottom left: A bear caught in Churchill is deported to the edge of Hudson Bay and released with the noise of exploding thunder flashes to scare the animal away. Many return to town the same day.

Right: Northern garbage dumps attract bears. A flame-singed female and her cubs pull food from the fire.

Left: Two bears meet and greet on the new-formed ice of Hudson Bay.

Above: When a big bear approaches, a small bear is all fear and hostility.

Right: A grouchy ancient bear, foreground, attacks a younger bear who wheels away.

Above: Two bear friends.

Left: Ptarmigan near low arctic willow bushes.

Right: A large male approaches in a friendly fashion, but a very hostile female goes to meet him.

THE SPIRIT BEARS

There is a cave in Switzerland, high in the Alps, 8,000 feet above sea level, formerly feared and avoided and known as the Drachenloch, the Dragon's Lair. Between 1917 and 1923 the German archeologist Emil Bächler excavated and explored the cave. Near the cave mouth, Neanderthal man had lived for untold generations some 75,000 years ago. As Bächler probed deeper into the remote recesses of the tunnel-like cave that ran far into the mountain, he found stone cists filled with cave bear skulls and thigh bones, and an altar-like stone slab. Arrayed upon it were seven bear skulls, all facing the entrance of the cave. Here, in the darkness of the Dragon's Lair, by the flickering light of oil lamps, Neanderthals worshiped the mighty cave bear, ancestor of both the polar bear and the brown bear. He was probably man's first god and, like an echo from the dawn of man, the cultic killing and veneration of the bear by most circumpolar people has persisted nearly to our day.

I walked once along the east coast of Lapland's Lake Inari on a glorious fall day, the birches aglow in silver and gold, the forest floor patina-green with reindeer moss. Pines, gnarled and troll-like, clung to rocky ridges. I sat on a boulder and watched the forest mirrored in the dark water of the lake and suddenly I had the uncanny feeling that in this remote wilderness someone was watching me. I turned and, in a rock niche behind me, staring out over the lake, was a bear skull, gray with age and speckled with lichen. Long ago, Lapps had killed the bear. They ate its meat with elaborate ritual, they buried its bones, they set its cleaned skull up in this holy place in the wilderness, and they assured the spirit of the bear with the ancient hunter's prayer for propitiation: "With the coming of next spring you will rise again and roam the hills . . . Pardon us now, forget that we have killed you."

And in the great Finnish national epic "Kalevala," the hunter promises the bear:

> Leave thy cold and cheerless dwelling
> . . . .
> Join thy friends in Kalevala.
> We shall never treat thee evil,
> Thou shalt dwell in peace and plenty,
> Thou shalt feed on milk and honey.

Left: A bear throws out his front legs to keep his balance.

Above: The sea steams in the intense cold of an early winter day in northwest Greenland.

Another time and on another continent, near the Cree Indian village of Eastmain on the east coast of James Bay, I found a bear skull lashed into a tree fork. Alonson Skinner, a traveler whose work was published in 1914 by the Ontario Historical Society, wrote that if a Cree hunter ". . . comes upon a bear and wishes to slay it, he first approaches and apologizes, explaining that nothing but the lack of food drives him to kill it, and begging that the bear will not be offended at him, nor permit the spirits of other bears to be angry." The dead bear was treated with the utmost respect and reverence, eaten in elaborate ceremony (the hunter ate the heart to acquire the bear's "cunning and courage"), the cleaned skull was painted with vermilion, the color of blood and life and resurrection, and "hung up on a tree in the forest."

Upon a remote Siberian beach, the Russian scientist S.M. Uspensky found polar bear skulls, carefully stacked in piles several feet high, where long ago arctic men prayed to the spirit of the bear. The Ket, a tribe of central Siberia, regarded the bear as their ancestor. They, too, set up the bear skull in the fork of a tree (as do the Ainu on Japan's Hokkaido Island, who still venerate the bear), and to this day the Ket call the bear *gyp*, "grandfather," or *qoi*, "stepfather."

Neanderthal man, Cro-Magnon man who came after him, and arctic man until recently, lived in the deeply mystic and spiritual world of the hunter who must kill in order to live. All animals, and man, the Inuit believed, had *inua*, "souls," and to ensure future hunting success and harmony with the spirits of nature, it was essential to placate the souls of slain animals, especially an animal as huge and man-like as the bear, who could stand upright, like an enormous hairy giant, or who, skinned, with his pinkish blubber, his finger-like claws and massive torso, looked gruesomely, horrifyingly like an immense naked human. "Life's greatest danger lies in the fact that man's food consists entirely of souls," an Igloolik Inuk told the Danish ethnologist Knud Rasmussen.

In this spiritual world of early man and arctic man, animals and humans were kin, an ancient belief reflected in totemism and in fables and mythology. It was a mental world where the real and the unreal, the factual and the spiritual, merged. A shaman of the Polar Inuit explained an unsuccessful polar bear hunt in an area where bears were usually numerous, like this: "The bears are not here, because there is no ice here, and there is no ice here, because the wind is too strong, and the wind is too strong because we have insulted the spirits."

It began with the now extinct cave bear, a mighty animal eight to nine feet long, that weighed about 1,500 pounds. It lived in the caves of Eurasia long before the coming of man. When Homo erectus occupied the great cave at Choukoutien near Beijing more than half a million years ago, bears lived in the cave already and were probably evicted with the help of man's first great special weapon, fire. Bears occupied the Drachenhöhle, the Dragon's Cave in Styria, Austria, for at least 10,000 years. The bones of about 50,000 bears were mined from this cave and ground into phosphate-rich fertilizer.

"Children show no trace of the arrogance which urges adult civilized men to draw a hard-and-fast line between their own nature and that of all other animals. Children have no scruples over allowing animals to rank as their full equals."

—Sigmund Freud

"In the first times . . . both people and animals lived on earth, but there was no difference between them."

—Nalungiaq, Netsilik Inuk talking to the Danish ethnologist Knud Rasmussen, 1924

Deep inside a cave near Montespan, France, in the foothills of the Pyrenees, Count Bégouen discovered the headless clay sculpture of a bear. Between its outstretched forelegs lay a cave bear skull. The sculpture was pierced by 30 spear holes and near it, in the once-soft clay of the cave floor, were the faint footprints of Ice Age hunters. Perhaps the hunters thrust their spears into the clay bear (the sculpture was then probably covered by a bear skin, the head affixed to it by a wooden peg) in the hope that by sympathetic magic their spears, in future hunts, would thus transfix the real bear. Or they may have practiced and enacted a hunt, as they chanted magic prayers and threw their weapons. Inuterssuaq, my mentor among the Polar Inuit of northwest Greenland, who with infinite patience explained to me the history and the customs of his people during the months I lived with him, told me that when he was young, his people made polar bears of snow and boys and young hunters attacked the snow bears and pierced them with spears.

Neanderthal man worshiped the bear, killed it and often, no doubt, was killed by it, for an enraged, three-quarter-ton cave bear with flashing three-inch canines and steel-hard finger-long claws was a terrifying adversary for men armed only with flint-tipped spears. At times, they buried bears and men with equal sorrow and ceremony. In a rectangular pit near Regourdu in southern France the bones of 20 bears were found. The grave was covered with a stone slab that weighed nearly a ton. To carry it would not have been difficult for several Neanderthal men, for they were bear-like in their strength. Short (about five feet tall) and squat, beetle-browed and bandy-legged, heavy-boned and powerfully muscled, Neanderthal men were perhaps the strongest humans that ever lived. According to the paleoanthropologist John Pfeiffer, "Their strongest individuals could probably lift weights of half a ton or so."

Sometimes bears and people were buried together and faint red traces suggest their remains may have been sprinkled with powdered ocher, the color of blood and life. Near Lascaux, France, with its magnificent cave paintings from Cro-Magnon times, a much older Neanderthal grave was discovered in 1961 and around the human skeleton lay the bones of more than 20 bears. That burial took place perhaps 50,000 or more years ago. But in the north, bear bones were brought to sacred caves until not too long ago. When the Russian scientists V.N. Chernetsov and W. Moszynska examined Shaytan, the Devil's Cave on the east slope of the Urals, they found its floor "covered with bones," for here "the Lozva Mansi [a Siberian tribe] made offerings . . . in comparatively recent times." Shaytan and other nearby caves "were used as burial places for the bear bones and here sacrifices were performed . . ." to appease the bears' spirits.

The polar bear was the ultimate bear—white, huge, mysterious. At King Island in Alaska's Bering Sea, the Jesuit missionary Bellarmine Lafortune noted in the 1930s, "A polar bear was hunted on foot and a hunter's greatest prestige came from his success as a polar bear hunter." It was an extremely risky hunt. The ice often drifted away and "many a King Islander, hot in pursuit of a polar

Until recently, Inuit hunted polar bears with sled dogs in a manner identical to the one shown in this engraving illustrating the travels of the 19th-century explorer Charles F. Hall. *Metropolitan Toronto Library*

bear, was cut off from his home in this way; some returned safely but others disappeared forever."

When a hunter returned with a bear, ancient ceremonies were observed to propitiate the bear's soul, for during all this time, the spirit of the great white bear hovered unseen, but strangely felt, about the village. If offended, it would depart in anger, and evil might strike the entire community. The bear's skull was taken to the *kagri*, the communal house, and placed upon a raised bench. It remained in this place of honor until the polar bear dance, "the most lavish of all King Island performances." Gifts were placed near the bear skull: skin scrapers, needle cases and *ulus*, the semi-lunar woman's knife, if the bear was a female, and a carving knife or drill, if the bear was a male. The gifts had their own spirits and essence, and these became the property of the bear's *inua*, its soul.

For four days for a male bear and five days for a female, the successful hunter fed the entire community dishes fixed by ancient tradition: *kacpadac*, sour greens with seal oil and reindeer tallow; *alluit*, snow with seal oil and berries; *tammoagac*, reindeer tallow, dry fish, seal oil and water. Then came the polar bear dance, the final act of atonement, and afterwards the bear's skull "was taken out on the moving ice, and when the ice made a noise as it moved, the spirit of the bear was regarded as having departed."

For nearly 2,000 years people of the Dorset culture held sway in most of North America's Arctic. The Inuit in their oral history that reaches far back into the beginnings of their people, still remember the Dorsets and call them Tunit, preternaturally powerful men who could haul a one-ton walrus across the ice as easily as an Inuk today pulls a small ringed seal, and so fast, they could run down and kill a caribou. They were probably the greatest artists that ever lived in the north. Their art is small, tiny figurines exquisitely carved from ivory. After man, notes the Canadian archeologist William E. Taylor, "bears are pre-eminent" in Dorset art. Despite their small size, George Swinton, a Canadian expert on Inuit art, has pointed out, Dorset carvings "exude intensity

"In East Greenland we have the mystic bear again as Tôrnârtik, the most prominent helping spirit."

—William E. Taylor, Canadian archeologist, 1967

After a successful polar bear hunt, Alaska's King Islanders propitiated the bear's spirit with a great feast and ". . . the most lavish of all King Island performances, Anirsaak, the polar bear dance."

—Bellarmine Lafortune, S.J., missionary on King Island, Alaska, 1934

and power," for these were very special carvings, magic carvings of magic bears, of ". . . Tôrnârssuk known as 'the master of the helping spirits,' who gave the shamans power."

The most famous of the Dorset spirit bears was found at Alernerk near the present village of Igloolik in the Canadian Arctic. It is carved from ivory, 6⅛ inches long, and it was made about 1,500 years ago. The bear's body is elongated. It seems to fly. It is incised with a stylized skeleton and in its neck is a tiny compartment with a sliding cover which once may have held red ocher. It probably depicts the spirit helper of a shaman.

To absorb the magic power of the bear, many Inuit wore amulets, most often a bear tooth as a pendant, identical to bear tooth pendants worn by Cro-Magnon men 30,000 years ago. The *angakoq*, the Inuit shaman, needed more; he wanted the bear's spirit to be his *tornaq*, his magic helper. It was a quest fraught with enormous danger. "If a shaman wishes to obtain a bear for his tornaq," Baffin Island Inuit told the American anthropologist Franz Boas in 1883, "he must travel alone to the edge of the land floe and summon the bears. Then a large herd will approach and frighten him almost to death. He falls down at once. Should he fall backwards he would die at once. If he falls upon his face, however, one bear out of the herd steps forward and asks him if he wishes him to become his tornaq." He takes the bear for his spirit and the two travel to his home. On the way, they pass a seal hole "and the bear captures the animal for his master. The Eskimo is now a great angakoq, and whenever he wants help he is sure to get it from his bear."

A polar bear heaves a block of ice at a walrus. It is an ancient belief in the north that bears occasionally kill walruses in this manner. Most scientists doubt it. *Metropolitan Toronto Library*

Polar bears and Inuit fascinated 19th-century travellers. This is how they imagined an encounter between an Inuk and a polar bear. *Metropolitan Toronto Library*

The bear spirit, the "flying bear" of Dorset art, could take the shaman to the moon, or deep into the sea, to seek help for his people from Sedna, the mother of seals and whales and walruses. And the bear spirit could protect his master from the powers of evil. In the long, Odyssey-like story of the great *angakoq* Kiviung, he is swept ashore in a strange land. A woman, Arnaitiang, lives there in a stone house, an evil witch who plans to eat him. But Kiviung "called his tornaq, a huge white bear, who arose roaring from under the floor of the house . . . As Kiviung kept on conjuring, the spirit came nearer and nearer to the surface," the witch trembled with fear and he escaped before she could trap him with her spells.

Most *angakut* were beneficial, men steeped in magic and mystery, who in trance and with the aid of their *tornait* tried to achieve balance and harmony between the world of spirits and the world of man. But some were evil men who used their powerful allies to deadly effect. The Pelly Bay Inuit told the anthropologist Asen Balikci in 1960 that "Moraq, a dangerous shaman, killed the brother of Itiioq, another shaman, with his tunraq [sic] polar bear." But the power thus unleashed for evil could become a "*tunraq kigdloretto*," a raving monster, blinded by frustration and hate, and totally out of control. "Utaq made a polar bear out of snow and turned it against Inutsaq," the Pelly Bay people told Balikci. "The blood-thirsty evil spirit turned back and later killed its own master."

Old men in the north still speak with respect of *nanook*, the great white bear. But the world of magic, when men and bear belonged to one realm, has ended. Southern man, whose culture swept the north and swept away its ancient beliefs, had no reverence for bears. To him the bear was a foe, or a curio to satisfy the age-old craving of the mighty for exotica. He caught the bear, baited it and often killed it with fiendish cruelty, and he slaughtered it in hecatombs to amuse the plebs. During one famous day in 237 A.D. in the Colosseum, while 50,000 spectators jeered and cheered, gladiators killed more than 1,000 bears, a spectacle sponsored by an immensely wealthy Roman who later became Emperor Gordian I.

"Everything is spirit. This is the essential thing for you to remember."

—The Polar Inuk Pualuna, talking to the French scientist Jean Malaurie, 1950

"To Eskimos, the polar bear is no longer a big, noble animal, a creature of folklore. They see dollar bills on him."

—Father Hubert Mascaret, missionary in the Canadian north, talking to the American writer Richard C. Davids, 1979

Polar bears are a common theme of Inuit art. This bear and seal was carved by Nalinek Temela of Lake Harbour on Baffin Island.

Overleaf: Whirling snow nearly hides a wandering bear.

Above: A parhelic circle and parhelia, mock suns, crystal-created sun halos in the Arctic.

Right: Clouds race across the sky in northwestern Greenland before a violent storm.

BEARS AT COURT

There were five treasures in the north that southern man desired: the ivory tusks of the walrus, the horn of the narwhal (the "unicorn's horn"), the tusks of the mammoth, the white gyrfalcon and, above all others, polar bears, *ursi albi*, the "white bears," as the Romans called them.

Brown bears were once common in Europe. Many cities were named after them, among them Bern and Berlin. They were hunted for sport, kept in bear pits, killed in arenas, and they were eaten. Bear steaks, lightly roasted, were a favorite Roman delicacy, and an unguent made of bear fat soothed the aching joints of rheumatic Romans. But bears were often infested with trichinae, a deadly parasite, and mortality among the bear-eating Roman elite was devastatingly high.

The north intrigued southern man and it repelled him. He was horrified by the frozen sea, "*mare concretum*," as Pliny put it so graphically, and by the terrible climate. "The whole of the country has so hard and severe a winter that there prevails there for eight months an altogether unsupportable cold," stated the Greek historian Herodotus about 430 B.C. But Herodotus wrote glowingly about the gorgeous furs that found their way from the remote, boreal land of the Issedones (Siberia) to the luxury-loving courts of the Middle East.

Somewhere in that murky, frigid north lived great white bears and early accounts of them range from the reasonably factual to the marvelously fanciful. Listing Greenland's animals, the anonymous author of the 13th-century Old Norse *Konungs Skuggsjá*, the King's Mirror, says: "There are bears, too . . . and they are white . . . and they wander most of the time about on the ice, hunting seals and whales . . ." Bishop Adam of Bremen in the *Gesta Hamburgensis*, the history of his see that reached far into the north, said in 1070 A.D. that in Norway there are "white bears . . . which live under water." And according to Hans Egede, the 18th-century "Apostle of Greenland," polar bears spend winter luxuriously in vast snow dens "made with pillars, like stately buildings."

Even in very remote times, by strange sea and land routes, a few polar bears reached the south. Ptolemy II, king of Egypt (285–246 B.C.) kept a polar bear at his private zoo and, reported the contemporary Greek writer Athenaeus who grew up in Egypt, on festive occasions the polar bear led a great procession through the streets of Alexandria, preceded by a group of men who carried a 180-foot-tall gilded phallus. The Romans with their vast network of animal

Left: Polar bear pelts were prized in the courts of Europe.

Above: A great male, so powerful he could kill a one-ton white whale and haul it out onto the ice.

dealers, who supplied the hundreds of thousands of victims that were killed in the circuses, occasionally obtained polar bears and pitted them against seals (probably the now nearly extinct Mediterranean monk seal) in aquatic battles staged in flooded arenas: ". . . *aequoreos ego cum certantibus ursi spectavi vitulos . . .*" ("sea calves also I beheld with bears pitted against them"), wrote the Roman poet Calpurnius in 57 A.D.

Polar bears came to the south by three main routes. One led from Siberia, and perhaps even Alaska, to China and Japan. Court annals for the year 858 A.D. record that two live polar bears were presented to the emperor of Japan. Bear skins and a few live bears from the north of Russia reached the Middle East and the courts of Europe via complex land and river routes. Most bears came to Europe after the Vikings discovered and settled Iceland in 860 A.D. and Greenland a century later.

Russia a thousand years ago was famed for its marvelous furs. In winter, fur fairs were held in the north, the greatest and most famous in Novgorod, and by 800 A.D. buyers arrived from as far away as the Persian Gulf. They traveled via Samarkand and continued north on frozen rivers by dog team. The Arab diplomat-merchant Ibn Fadlan was greatly impressed in Novgorod with the people who arrived from the far north with their furs. "As soon as the hunter buckles boards eight or nine ells long to his feet . . . he conquers the greyhounds in running," he reported in 922 A.D. to his master, Muktedir, the caliph of Baghdad. The hunters came on skis! Of all the skins brought from the north, those of polar bears were the rarest and the most highly prized. "These bear skins are soft, and they are brought to the Egyptian lands as gifts," noted the 13th-century Arab traveler and geographer Ibn Sa'id.

In the south these pelts were worth a fortune, but the arctic hunters were poorly paid. In 1556 the English explorer Steven Burrough tried to reach the river Ob. Near the island of Novaya Zemlya in the Barents Sea, he met Samoyed hunters who had killed three walruses and a polar bear. For each walrus tusk they received a ruble and for "one white bear skin . . . three robles." By then the export of polar bears and polar bear skins had become an imperial monopoly in Russia. When England's Muscovy Company asked Richard Gray, its agent in Moscow, to send them live polar bears in 1558, he regretfully informed them that he could not send "any white bears . . . [for none] may pass out of the realme without a special licence from the Emperour." The Russians loved the luxurious pelts. The English explorer Anthony Jenkinson spent some time in Moscow in 1557 and described the city and its people in detail: "The Russe, if he be a man of any abilitie, never goeth out of his house in the winter, but upon his sled . . . and in his sled he sits upon . . . a white Beares skinne . . ."

In 860 A.D. the Norsemen discovered and later settled Iceland, and in 986 Eirik the Red and about 400 settlers founded the first Viking colony in Greenland. They were essentially subsistence farmers. They kept sheep and scrawny cattle and to them polar bears were both a menace and a blessing. Nearly every

The Samoyeds of northern Russia, now called Nentsi, were primarily reindeer herders. Those who lived near the arctic coast also hunted polar bears and walruses. *Metropolitan Toronto Library*

For his christening in Prague in 1619 Prince Rupert of the Rhine (later first governor of the Hudson's Bay Company) received lavish gifts "borne in coaches drawn by trained polar bears and tame black stags."

—Peter C. Newman, Canadian author, in his book *Company of Adventurers*, 1985

"Combat vigoureux" is the title of this 1791 engraving, which pits a polar bear against a Finnmark (arctic Norway) hunter. *Metropolitan Toronto Library*

The polar bears at the court of Denmark "would have lived [in the water] for whole days without difficulty, if they had not been brought up by cords and chains to which they were fastened."

—Isaac de la Peyrère, author, Copenhagen, 1644

summer, polar bears that had been hunting seals far out upon the pack ice were swept ashore, together with the melting floes, upon the north and west coasts of Iceland by the East Greenland Current and the Irminger Current. Famished after their long drift ("they become furious with hunger," said the French writer Isaac de la Peyrère in 1644), the bears killed sheep and cattle and sometimes settlers. In 1274, the Iceland annals report, 22 polar bears were killed and the next year 27. In 1321, a bear killed eight people. On the other hand, live bears and even bear pelts were extremely valuable. About 880 A.D. Ingimundr the Old captured two bear cubs after killing their mother, sailed jubilantly to Norway and presented the bears to King Harold the Fairhaired who rewarded him with an ocean-going ship filled with a cargo of timber.

Some of Iceland's earliest laws dealt with the problems of polar bears. A man who owned a tame bear had to treat it like a dog and he had to pay compensation for all damages caused by the bear. But if anyone harmed a captive polar bear, except in self-defence, he had to pay a hefty indemnity to the owner.

Eirik the Red, too, had trouble with a polar bear. Thorgil, an adventurous Viking and devout Christian, spent the winter at Brattahlid, Eirik's farm in southwest Greenland. "A bear made inroads on men's stock," the *Flóamanna Saga* recounts, "and a price was set on the bear's head." Eirik did not like it. He was a pagan and felt the ancient Nordic reverence for bears. One day the bear caught Thorgil's son "and played with him." Thorgil heard the boy cry, grabbed his sword, raced to the bear and "smote it between the ears with all his strength and passion, splitting the beast's skull right through, so that it fell down dead." Eirik, it was said, was furious, for he "had put an evil trust in the creature."

Greenland's Viking settlements were rarely visited by polar bears. They were too far south for the ice-loving, seal-eating bears. To pay for costly imports —wood, grain, iron, clothes, malt, wine, church vestments and ornaments— the Norse made *nordrsetur*, hunting trips to the farthest north, to obtain walrus tusks, gyrfalcon, narwhal tusks and polar bears. The 17th-century Icelandic author Bjørn Jonsson in his *Annals of Greenland*, based on old sources, wrote: "All the landowners in Greenland had great ships built for . . . Nordrsetur, furnished with all manner of hunting gear . . ." They rowed and sailed far north through ice-choked seas into Melville Bay and perhaps as far as Ellesmere Island. In 1266, hunters from Gardar, the main settlement, ventured farther north than ever before and emerged from dense fog near a shore with "many glaciers and seals and white bears." The next year they returned and this time there were so many polar bears that "they could not land because of the bears."

Polar bears became instruments of diplomacy or, in less flattering terms, high class bribes. It was the ambition of an Icelander named Isleifr to become a bishop. When a young polar bear arrived on one of the trading ships from Greenland, he bought it and sent it in 1054 A.D. to the Holy Roman Emperor Henry III, who graciously made Isleifr a bishop. The bear was the wonder of the emperor's court and one man who watched this with envy was Bishop Bruno of

From the north came polar "bear skins that are soft, and they are brought to Egyptian lands as gifts."

—Ibn Sa'id, 13th-century Arab traveler and geographer

Egisheim. When he became Pope Gregory IX, he sent an urgent message to Iceland, asking for a live polar bear. None were available and the Icelanders sent the pope instead the skin of a very large polar bear.

The Greenlanders, too, wanted a bishop. They sent one of their wisest men, Einar Sokkason, to King Sigurd of Norway. To bolster his plea, Sokkason took walrus tusks along and a live polar bear. He gave the ivory tusks to the king but cagily held onto the bear until the priest Arnald had been consecrated first bishop of Greenland in 1125. Only then did Sokkason present the king with the "polar bear he had brought with him."

Live polar bears were precious. The Icelander Audun visited Greenland, bought there a bear "with all his worldly goods" and in 1064 A.D. presented it to King Svend II of Denmark, who gave him money to make a pilgrimage, a magnificent ring, a leather sock filled with silver and a ship plus cargo.

It was then widely believed that polar bears ate mainly fish. In the 13th-century *Geographia Universalis* by an unknown author, it says: ". . . white bears, that . . . take fish under the ice . . . they carry them to shore and live on them . . ." Because of this belief, arrangements were made for bears kept at royal courts to catch fish. King Henry III of England (1207–1272) ordered "the sheriffs of London to furnish six pence a day to support our White Bear in our Tower of London; and to provide a muzzle and iron chain to hold him when he was fishing in the Thames."

King Henry's bear was a gift from Haakon Haakonsson of Norway. King Haakon, who had just become suzerain of Iceland and Greenland, was in an ideal position to obtain polar bears, and he sent some as gifts to fellow monarchs. Polar bears were probably taken to Spain and to the court at Tunis, in north Africa. But one polar bear in particular made a strange journey. It was caught in Greenland, shipped to Iceland and from there to King Haakon in Norway. He presented the bear to the Holy Roman Emperor Frederick II whose court was then in Sicily. In 1233, Frederick sent a delegation with precious gifts to the Sultan El-Kamil in Damascus. Among them was the polar bear from northern Greenland, and it is recorded that in the early mornings its keepers took it on a long rope to catch fish in the palm-fringed Barada River.

Left: Inuit skin the huge body of a bear with speed and precision, careful not to nick the valuable hide.

Right: Dutch whalers often hunted polar bears. Occasionally, as shown in this print, polar bears also hunted Dutch whalers. *Metropolitan Toronto Library*

Above: The northwest coast of Greenland mirrored in a calm late summer sea.

Left: Prized by princes and potentates of many lands, the white gyrfalcon was the most precious bird of the north.

Right: Polar bears stand easily on their hind legs.

Above: "The ever-wandering-one," Inuit call the bear in their poems. Some bears travel far. Most bears, though, belong to discrete regional populations.

Right: A bear spreads out upon the snow to cool off after a play-fight.

Above: Hoarfrost rimes the willow bushes along Hudson Bay in early winter.

Right: In medieval times, the narwhal's tusk, thought to be the unicorn's horn, was worth many times its weight in gold.

Opposite: This bear is partly curious, partly suspicious.

BEARS AND EXPLORERS

The Inuit were hunting polar bears on the ice of the Northwest Passage. The two men, Akpaleeapik and Akeeagok, and their sons, Iseechee and Seeglook, and I, had left Grise Fiord on Ellesmere Island three weeks ago in April, 1967. We sledged along the soaring, snow-streaked, burnt sienna cliffs of southern Ellesmere Island and crossed Jones Sound, skirting house-high pressure ridges. We saw many bear tracks and a few bears. But the animals escaped into the chaos of pressure ice, scaling effortlessly 15-foot-high, upthrust, wind-polished ice floes with crampon-sharp claws and skid-proof soles. When we crossed Devon Island, our sled dogs were starving. Vicious storms pinned us down in foodless valleys; our dogs had nothing to eat for seven days.

On Lancaster Sound our fortunes improved. This is the richest sea mammal region in Canada with about 1,000 walruses, 10,000 narwhals, 10,000 white whales, ringed seals, bearded seals and harp seals. After extensive aerial surveys in 1979, the biologist Ray Schweinsburg of the Northwest Territories Wildlife Service estimated that there are at least 1,000 polar bears in the Lancaster Sound area. Within a week Akpaleeapik and Akeeagok shot four large bears. Our famished sled dogs gulped down bear meat and fat in frantic haste, each dog devouring 10 to 15 pounds. They then curled up in bloated bliss and were useless as either sled dogs or hunting dogs for the next 12 hours. We ate the dark stringy bear meat as a thick stew, well boiled to kill any trichinae that could have caused the excruciatingly painful and often fatal trichinosis. Studies in Greenland have shown that about 30 percent of all polar bears are infested with trichinae (and 66 percent of all sled dogs).

Now we were camped near Beechey Island, which the geographer Andrew Taylor has called "the most historic spot in the Queen Elizabeth Islands." Here Inuit and men from the south had pursued their divergent dreams. To the Inuit long ago, as to our group now, the ice that covered the sea formed an essential highway, and polar bears and sea mammals were their vital food. We camped repeatedly near the remnants of prehistoric Inuit Thule culture homes, built with the bones of their main prey, the bowhead whale. Among the ribs that once had formed house rafters, Iseechee found the age-bleached skull of a polar bear, the trophy of a successful hunt perhaps 500 years ago. To the Inuit this was *nunassiaq*, the "beautiful land" where, as the American explorer Elisha Kent Kane observed, "every rock had its name, every hill its significance." They

Left: The tracks of a polar bear patrolling his icy realm.

Above: At the time Europeans discovered America, polar bears ranged much farther south than they do today.

Whaling and bear hunting near
Spitsbergen in the early 18th century.
Metropolitan Toronto Library

gloried in its animal wealth, which was their food, and they revered this harsh land for "The earth and everything belonging to it . . . are sacred," the Netsilingmiut told the Danish ethnologist Knud Rasmussen.

To men from the south, for many centuries, the Arctic was merely a monstrous but surely not insuperable obstacle in their obsessive search for a northern sea route to the immense wealth of the East, for a Northeast or Northwest Passage to Cathay and Zipangu (Japan). Ice, cold and scurvy were their enemies, and polar bears were an additional menace of the north. They pursued their quest with fierce determination and a marvelous optimism based on ignorance, and they often paid for it with suffering and death. Behind us, infinitely lonely in the fulvous light of night, beneath a pale-yellow sun flanked by even paler mock suns, were graves of men of the Franklin expedition who had died here more than a century ago, young men from England, poorly dressed and poorly prepared, battling the Arctic to find the Northwest Passage, pursuing southern man's dream of wealth and fame.

The Northeast and Northwest passages as economically viable routes eluded them, but they did explore and open the Arctic. In their wake came the whalers, who destroyed much of the Arctic's wildlife wealth and brought disease and death to its long-isolated natives. The entrance to the Northwest Passage, where we now hunted polar bears, had been discovered by William Edward Parry of Britain's Royal Navy in late July of 1819. Parry was delighted. This was an arctic Eden, the "headquarters of the whales." Walruses lay "huddled together, like pigs" and were "stupidly tame." Giant bowhead whales lolled in the dark sea. On July 30, they saw 89. (Today only about 200 bowhead whales survive in the entire eastern Arctic.) Ivory-tusked narwhals were "very numerous" and white whales "were swimming about the ships in great numbers." Polar bears ambled across the ice floes. The sailors tried to lassoo them and killed some with boarding lances. It was part of a pattern that prevailed for several hundred years. The explorers and whalers who came into these pristine regions killed the bears and sometimes the bears killed them.

"The True and perfect Description of three voyages to . . . Noua Zembla . . . where neuer any man has bin before; with the cruell Beares, and other Monsters of the Sea . . ."

—Title of the 1609 book describing the three voyages of the Dutch explorer Willem Barents

These old engravings show some of the animals the whalers encountered in the north. *Above:* the harp seal, a walrus and its calf, and a Greenland shark. *Below:* the bowhead of the arctic seas was the "right whale" for the whalers: slow, timid and immensely fat. It carried in its mouth about 350 valuable baleen plates. The cachalot, or sperm whale, was hunted in warmer seas. *Metropolitan Toronto Library.*

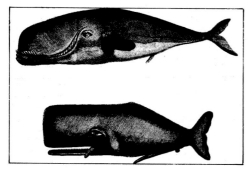

For frequent and deadly encounters between man and polar bears, the expeditions of Willem Barents stand out. In 1594, Barents, a veteran navigator, was asked by the Dutch States General to find the Northeast Passage. He was so certain of success, he carried with him trunkloads of religious tracts to give to the pagans of Cathay. On July 9, 1594, north of Russia near Novaya Zemlya they saw a polar bear in the water and shot at it with a musket, but the bear "shewed most wonderful strength" and swam on. The sailors tried to lassoo the bear and take it alive to their ship "to haue shewed her for a strange wonder in Holland; but she vsed such force, that they were glad that they were rid of her . . ." The bear climbed into their boat. The frantic sailors managed to kill it with a pike and "brought the skinne to Amsterdam."

Officers and sailors of that time were keen to kill polar bears because the skins were valuable, but their muskets were unreliable and inadequate for this hunt. When the English explorer John Davis sailed south along the Baffin Island coast in 1585, he saw near Cape Walsingham ". . . white beares . . . of a monstruous bignesse." One bear slept. Davis shot but the flint "missed fire." The bear merely ". . . looked up, and layed downe his head againe." Davis took another musket and shot two bullets into the animal's head. The bear was only "amazed." The sailors finally killed it with boar spears.

On September 9, 1594, Barents's men landed on a small island north of Russia to pick up "diamonds" (rock crystal). Tired after a long walk, their haversacks loaded with crystal, two of the Dutch sailors lay down on the beach to sleep when, as Gerrit de Veer, the chronicler of the expeditions reported, "a great leane white beare came sodainely stealing out, and caught one of them fast by the necke, who not knowing what it was . . . cried out, Who is it that pulles me so by the necke? wherewith the other . . . perceiuing it to be a monsterous beare, cryed and said, Oh mate, it is a beare! . . . and ran away. The beare . . . bit [the sailor's] head in sunder and suckt out his blood."

Twenty men came from the ships to drive the bear away from the body. They attacked the animal with muskets and pikes, but the bear "fiercely and cruelly ran at them, and gat another of them . . . which she tare in peeces, wherewith all the rest ran away." Additional men arrived from the ships and, now more than 30, they attacked the bear again. They fired "three times and mist." The purser then shot the bear "into the head betweene both the eyes, and yet she held the man still fast by the necke, and lifted up her head, with the man in her mouth . . ." They killed the bear with pikes and halberds and, as it says so often in the expedition accounts, ". . . tooke her skinne to Amsterdam." The remains of the sailors were buried on the arctic beach where they had been killed.

In 1596, Barents tried again to breach the Northeast Passage. This time ice pinned his ship against the coast of Novaya Zemlya and crushed it. Until then, no Europeans had ever survived an arctic winter. The Dutch sailors built a large house of driftwood logs, fended off inquisitive or aggressive polar bears, killed some of them and ate their meat and liver and were the first Europeans to discover the fact, well known to the natives of the north, that polar bear liver is exceedingly toxic. It contains so much vitamin A, that those who eat it can die of hypervitaminosis, or at least become extremely sick.

While the men were busy constructing their log house, there came a bear that "desired to tast a peece of some of vs." They killed it with lances "but her death did us more hurt than her life . . . [for] we drest her liuer and eate it, which in the taste liked us well, but it made vs all sicke . . ." Three men were so sick "we verily thought that we should haue lost them, for all their skins came of from foote to the head . . ." Nearly three centuries later, the American explorer Dr. Elisha Kent Kane wrote in his diary on October 8, 1854, that "I satisfied myself that it was a vulgar superstition to regard the liver of the polar bear as poisonous. I ate of it freely . . . and today I have the symptoms of poison in full measure . . . vertigo, diarrhoea, and their concomitants." In 1906, Peter Freuchen, Alfred Wegener and 17 other members of the Danish expedition to East Greenland ate polar bear liver and became terribly sick. They vomited frequently, their eyesight became severely impaired, they had diarrhea and "after a while their skin began to peel."

All fall and winter Barents's men were harried by bears. Some were collecting firewood when three bears approached. The men ran, the bears followed. They saved themselves "by throwing billets [of wood] and other things at them, and every time we threw they ran after them, as a dogge vseth to doe at a stone that is cast to him." In winter, when it was so cold the clock stopped, the wine froze "and the very clothes upon our backs were white all over with frost and icicles," the bears laid siege to their dwelling. One "beare came bouldly toward the house and came downe the staires close to the dore seeking to breake into the house . . . and made such a roaring that it was fearefull to heare . . ." The 11 survivors of this expedition reached Russia in two open boats.

Their stories dampened Dutch enthusiasm for the Northeast Passage. But their reports, and those of English navigator Henry Hudson who sailed to Spitsbergen in 1607, of arctic seas alive with giant bowhead whales—"which whale is the best of all sorts," England's Muscovy Company happily noted— encouraged the merchants of Europe to invest vast sums in arctic whaling. Soon 500 to 600 Dutch, German, English and French whaling ships, with 20,000 men or more, sailed to the Spitsbergen region each year, warships accompanying the fleets of each nation. In slightly more than a century, the Dutch alone killed 60,000 bowhead whales. (The whales never recovered from this slaughter. Even now they are exceedingly rare in this region.)

To establish early whaling rights by their presence, the Dutch sent seven sailors each to winter on the small island of Jan Mayen and on Spitsbergen. All the men on Jan Mayen died. The Spitsbergen crew survived and one of them, Jacob van der Brugge, kept a diary (published in Amsterdam in 1634) with extensive observations of the polar bears. The bears began to arrive in late

Walruses like togetherness. They sleep packed tightly together, either on land or on ice floes.

Polar bears "are at constant enmity with the Walrus . . . frequently both the combatants perish in the conflict."

—Thomas Pennant, author of
Arctic Zoology, London, 1784

November and December. By January (1634) ". . . the bears were continuously stopping near our tent [really a log cabin], for we were scarcely free of them for two or three hours . . . [and they made] a terrible noise by their growling." On cold and stormy days, van der Brugge accurately observed, the bears dug pits into the snow "to sleep in."

As the winter progressed, the bears became hungrier and more aggressive. They ate seaweed: "We observed that the bears had clawed up much rock-weed and big leaves;" they walked along the beach in large groups "like cattle in the Netherlands," and occasionally the bears fought fiercely with one another. On March 22, 1634 (at the time of the bears' mating season), the sailors saw "fourteen or sixteen bears together on the coast, who were having a great fight." The sailors killed 29 bears that winter and took their skins and two live cubs to Amsterdam.

Forty years later when the Hamburg merchant Friedrich Martens visited the "whale fishery" in Spitsbergen, polar bear killing had become part of the whaling business. The thousands of "carcasses of whales" attracted the bears, "and near them we killed the most." The skins, treated with heated sawdust "which sucks up the fat," were taken to Germany and "are very comfortable to those that travel in winter." Bear fat was rendered into oil and used in "lamps, where it does not stink so much as the train-oyl [whale oil]." The fat "of their feet melted out, is used for pain of the limbs; it is also given to women in travail, to bring away the child; it causes also a plentiful sweat . . ." But the whalers rarely ate polar bear meat because they believed that "it makes their hair grey." The bears, on the other hand, frequently ate the whalers. Hundreds of men died in the north and were taken to a small island known to this day as Deadman Island. There, reported Martens, "the dead are laid in coffins and well covered over with great rocks. Afterwards the white bears find them and devour them."

Such stories strongly influenced Europe's perception of the polar bears. In the popular imagination, the bears became evil incarnate, ghouls and demons of the north, and for a long time the "white-shrouded bear," as Herman Melville called him in *Moby Dick*, remained the essence of horror and evil. "In a state of nature . . . they are of dreadful ferocity," wrote English naturalist Thomas Pennant in 1784 in his two-volume *Arctic Zoology*. "They seem to give a preference to human blood; and will greedily disinter the graves of the buried . . ." Lacking humans, Pennant noted, polar bears eat "fish, seals, and the carcasses of whales. They also take deer [reindeer], hares, young birds, eggs and often whortleberries and crowberries." Eighteenth-century polar bear biology was a strange mélange of fact and fiction.

At the time Europeans discovered America, polar bears (and Inuit) ranged much farther south than they do today. The climate was colder than it is now (it was the time of the Little Ice Age when, noted the diarist Samuel Pepys, it was so cold that during their winter "Frost Fairs" Londoners roasted oxen on the frozen Thames). The ice covering the sea was more extensive and the ice-loving seals were more numerous. Polar bears were common along the Labrador coast, they hunted harp seals on the spring ice off Newfoundland, and the French explorer Samuel de Champlain claimed (perhaps mistakenly) in 1626 when he reached the large Anticosti Island in the Gulf of St. Lawrence that "it is not inhabited by the natives [Indians or Inuit] because of the number of very dangerous white bears that are to be found on it."

Compared with the lurid accounts of polar bears in the European Arctic, the polar bears found on the North American coast appeared timid, well-fed and were rarely aggressive. The French explorer Jacques Cartier left St. Malo in France with two ships and 61 men on April 20, 1534, and in May reached Funk Island near Newfoundland. On the "Isle des Ouaiseaulx," the island of birds, the now extinct great auk bred in "numbers so great as to be incredible . . . all the ships of France might load a cargo of them without one perceiving that any had been removed . . . And these birds are so fat that it is marvelous . . .

Near Newfoundland "we captured [a polar bear] by main force. His flesh was as good to eat as that of a two-year-old heifer."

—Jacques Cartier, French explorer, 1534

"The polar bear is an intelligent and crafty animal, but it is cursed with intense curiosity . . ."

—Fridtjof Nansen, Norwegian explorer, 1883

"We . . . saw many bears going in troops, like the cattle in the Netherlands."

—Seven Dutch whalers wintering on Spitsbergen, 1633–34

"... salmon innumerable, continually leaping into the air, had attracted a great concourse of [polar] bears."

—George Cartwright, British trader, Labrador, 1778

"... when wee came neere the shore [of Baffin Island], wee found ... white beares of a monstruous bignesse."

—John Davis, English explorer, 1585

"The beare at first faling vpon the man, bit his head in sunder and suckt out his blood."

—Gerrit de Veer, description of Willem Barents's 1594 expedition in search of the Northeast Passage

Notwithstanding that the island lies 14 leagues [31 miles] from shore, bears swim out to it from the mainland in order to feed on these birds; and our men found one as big as a calf and as white as a swan that sprang into the sea in front of them."

French and English explorers found the polar bears delicious. Cartier said the meat was as good as that of "a two-year-old heifer." Anthony Parkhurst, a Bristol merchant and explorer, found in 1577 in Newfoundland "plentie of Beares every where ... and their flesh is as good as yong beefe ..." Richard Hore, a wealthy London leather merchant during the reign of King Henry VIII, organized the first tourist trip to America. He set out with "six score persons, whereof 30 were gentlemen. . . ." Along the Newfoundland coast they "saw store of beares both blacke and white of whome they killed some, and tooke them for no badde foode." The bears were enormously fat from eating salmon and were considered harmless. Said Parkhurst: "I beleeve assuredly they would not hurt any body unless they be forced."

Polar bears and salmon were immensely numerous on the Labrador coast. George Cartwright, an English "sportsman," trapper and trader, lived in Labrador for 16 years (1770–86) and his diaries are full of ecstatic descriptions of fish and bears. In 1778 he visited White Bear River. The pool beneath its 14-foot waterfall was packed with salmon and the "shores were strewed with the remains of thousands of salmon which had been killed by the white bears." It was a beautiful spot. Alder and birch flanked the sparkling rapids and the waterfall and "salmon innumerable, continually leaping into the air, had attracted a great concourse of bears." Some dove into the pool and emerged with salmon; others grabbed salmon in the shallow rapids. "Others again were walking along the shore; some were going into the woods and others coming out." Cartwright "counted thirty-two white bears and three black ones." He shot six of them and would have shot more had he not run out of ammunition. The warming climate in the late 19th and in the 20th century and intensive hunting destroyed the animals. Now polar bears have vanished from the Labrador coast.

In the American Arctic, the Spitsbergen pattern repeated itself. Explorers opened the north and shot a few bears. Whalers and sealers followed and killed thousands of them. From the huge bowhead whale, the whalers took only baleen and blubber. The "kreng," as they called the giant, wasted carcass, was cut adrift. On July 27, 1823, all along the landfast ice east of Bylot Island in the Canadian Arctic, the men of the whaling ship *Cumbrian* saw "the dead bodies of hundreds of flenched whales ... the air for miles around was tainted with the foetor which arose from such masses of putridity." Such smells attracted polar bears from a vast region. In 1864 in Baffin Bay the whaling ship *Constantia* came across a "dead whale covered with bears. The ship's crew shot sixty ... [and recovered] forty-five." Dead whales, whaling ships and whalers naturally attracted hungry or curious polar bears. On a foggy day in 1875, the men of the *Victor* were playing football on the Baffin Bay ice, when suddenly a polar bear joined them, eagerly chasing the sealskin ball. He had, in seconds, the field to himself.

As the whales declined, the whalers probed ever farther into the arctic seas. By the 1890s they had reached Banks Island in the western Arctic which Inuit, long ago, used to call "the land of the white bear." The whaling captain Hartson H. Bodfish approached Banks Island in August, 1902, and "Forty to fifty polar bears watched us from the cliffs as we steamed past . . . We killed a great many of these animals, using the meat chiefly for dog food."

The great whales that once surged through the arctic seas in vast numbers were now exceedingly rare, and the whalers killed everything that could be sold for profit. The deep-pile, silky-soft polar bear pelts were popular in Europe; thousands of pudgy Victorian babies were photographed on polar bear rugs. Between 1905 and 1909, Dundee whalers alone killed more than a thousand polar bears on the ice off East Greenland, in Davis Strait and Hudson Bay. Inuit continued to hunt the bears as their ancestors had done for untold millennia. And long after the whalers left the Arctic where they had killed much of the wildlife, sportsmen came from the south to kill the remaining bears.

Dogs hold a bear at bay while a fur-clad whaler shoots the animal. Polar bear pelts were highly prized in 19th-century Europe. *Metropolitan Toronto Library*

Muskox herd in defensive position. Like the polar bears, they, too, were powerless against the guns of European hunters.

"Flagged trees," near the coast of
Hudson Bay, are formed by strong winds
and ice spicules.

Above: A Polar Inuk of northwest Greenland travels in a snowstorm to hunt seals at the floe edge, the limit of landfast ice.

Right: Whalers from many countries hunted in the Arctic. This Danish whaler was buried on Herschel Island in Canada's western Arctic.

Above: To jump or not to jump. Confronted by a cleft in the ice, a bear hesitates, estimates — and then jumps.

Left: A frozen-in iceberg off the northwest coast of Greenland.

Top left: Belugas, or white whales, are whales of the Arctic. Occasionally ice traps them in a bay and then polar bears succeed in killing them.

Centre left: A huge Kodiak bear catches salmon in an Alaskan river. Polar bears, long ago, caught salmon in similar fashion in Labrador streams.

Bottom left: A bear breaks the ice by pounding it with stiff front legs. He extracts seaweed from the shallow water.

Right: Powerful and belligerent, the ivory-tusked walrus is more than a match for the polar bear.

THE HUNT OF THE GREAT WHITE BEAR

Eighteen thousand years ago, at the height of the last Ice Age, when mile-thick glaciers covered much of Europe, Stone Age hunters lived at a site in northern Russia now known as Byzovaia, near the Pechora River, just 100 miles south of the Arctic Circle. Their camp was close to the Ural Ice Cap. It was intensely cold and to survive they must have been dressed in well-sewn fur clothing, similar perhaps to the clothing that enabled Inuit to live in the Arctic. They hunted the large mammals of the region. The 422 bones found by Russian scientists at this most northerly Paleolithic site in European Russia are of mammoth, reindeer and polar bear. The site, notes the archeologist Robin W. Dennell of the University of Sheffield, "records the earliest known encounter between humans and polar bears."

As man spread north and east from central Europe and Asia to the shores of the Arctic Ocean, crossed Bering Strait 10,000 years ago and settled the vast coastline of the North American Arctic and Greenland, he began to hunt the great white bear that gave him food and fur and fame. It was a primal struggle between man and bear, with the odds in favor of the man because he was, as the Bible says of Esau, "a cunning hunter." Man used trained dogs (huskies were probably hunting dogs before they also became sled dogs) to stop the bear and hold him at bay. The hunter was armed only with a spear, the four- to five-foot-long shaft of wood (or of spliced bone or antler in regions where driftwood was rare), tipped with stone, ivory or, in parts of Alaska, with polished jade. As the enraged bear lunged at the snarling, howling huskies, the man rushed in, tried to drive his spear deep into the side of the bear, then jumped aside as the wounded bear, 800 pounds of fury and power, turned on him. One slip, one small mistake, and the man was dead, because despite its lumbering appearance, the bear is very fast and agile, its strength is awesome, and it can easily kill the hunter with one blow or bite.

Grise Fiord Inuit told the Canadian anthropologist Milton R. Freeman that in May, 1970, white whales, trapped by vast ice fields near the coast of Ellesmere Island, were discovered by a 300-pound female bear. She killed two adult whales, each weighing about 2,000 pounds, yanked them out of the water and dragged one of them more than 20 feet across the ice. In Churchill in 1972, two captured white whales destined for the Minneapolis zoo, were kept in a holding tank near the Churchill River. A 500-pound bear killed one whale, pulled the

Left: An "inukshuk," a man-shaped cairn built long ago by Inuit as a marker in the featureless land.

Above: A bear in repose appears all round and a bit phlegmatic. But when he charges, he can be lightning quick and deadly.

"*February ninth [1938] . . . I saw a polar bear. I killed it; I was so happy thinking that the children would have something to eat, that I never forgot that day. I had killed a male white bear, big and fat.*"

— Nuligak, Inuk hunter, in his memoirs
   I, Nuligak

A husky jumps to safety as the bear attacks. Inuit use trained dogs to hold the bear at bay. They haul the bear they have killed back to camp themselves or harness a dog team to pull it.

Boys and men among the Polar Inuit of northwest Greenland wear pants made of polar bear fur.

700-pound carcass across the four-foot-high rim of the tank and hauled it 50 feet away "as easily as if it had been a sardine," according to an Indian who witnessed the killing.

The polar bear, wrote the Norwegian explorer Fridtjof Nansen, who faced and killed many bears, ". . . can be surprisingly swift. It can jump almost as a cat does. . . ." The Canadian biologist Gordon Stenhouse, testing polar bear deterrents, surrounded the tower at Cape Churchill with a four-and-a-half-foot-high wire fence. A bear squeezed through beneath, Stenhouse shot at it with a riot control rubber bullet, the startled bear wheeled and cleared the fence in a flying leap. At the Zurich, Switzerland, zoo, to the consternation of its director, Heini Hediger, a polar bear jumped out of a moat by scaling a ten-foot-high vertical wall. "No one had considered this possible before it happened," wrote Hediger. In Churchill, where bears come into town and are sometimes chased by cars, young males have been clocked at speeds of more than 35 mph.

This then was the animal arctic man pursued, alone and with his puny spear, an animal of enormous strength that hunted its main prey, seals, with a lethal combination of cunning, stealth and speed. To hunt polar bears required immense courage and endurance. In 1967, the Inuit Akpaleeapik and Akeeagok with whom I traveled, hunted a bear through jagged, upthrust pressure ice on Jones Sound. Akeeagok ran far ahead of the sled with a few brief rests, for nine hours—and he did not get the bear! The survivors of American Charles Francis Hall's expedition wintered near Etah in northwest Greenland in 1873. One evening a polar bear passed their camp and an elderly Polar Inuk, Awatok, immediately set out in pursuit with his sled, a team of dogs and a four-foot spear as his weapon. He remained out all night in a northeast gale with a temperature of −30° F. Late the next day he returned with the bear's carcass on his sled. The old man quietly entered the expedition camp and when he "took off his jacket to dry it, his back, marked with the scars of what appeared to be frightful wounds, showed that he had previously had fights with the same enemy."

There are few men today who know what it is like to face an infuriated bear armed only with a spear. One is Utûniarssuaq, a Polar Inuk with whom I lived and traveled. He was a small man, barely five feet tall, roundish, gentle, with large horn-rimmed glasses that gave him a deceptively studious look. At 61, he was one of the most skilful and enduring hunters of the region. One day in 1971 he talked of early hunts, when he was "young and strong."

He had sledged to catch dovekies, starling-sized seabirds, with a long-handled scoop net when he came across fresh polar bear tracks. He had no gun, harpoon or spear. He lashed his snow knife to the net handle and went after the bear. As soon as he was close, he released his dogs. They overtook and stopped the bear. "I ran up to him," said Utûniarssuaq, his eyes gleaming with the excitement of the remembered hunt. "He saw me and charged. The dogs bit his rear and when he turned, I dashed in and pushed the knife into his side. He was nearly on top of me then; I could feel his breath on my face. But he turned

"Kuvlu noted from the tracks exactly what each bear had been doing, and, with intense concentration, inferred the behavior of the animals . . . In this way the Eskimo learns to understand his prey."

—Richard K. Nelson, American anthropologist, Wainwright, Alaska, 1960s again for the dogs, and then I came from below and pushed the spear into his chest. And so I killed the bear and that was south of Thule a long long time ago."

It was a fight to the death between males. No one expressed it better than Orpingalik, an old Netsilik Inuk, in his poem recorded in the early 1920s by Knud Rasmussen:

It threw me down
Again and again,
Then breathless departed
And lay down to rest,
Hid by a mound on the floe.
Heedless it was, and unknowing
That I was to be its fate.
Deluding itself
That he alone was a male
And unthinking
That I too was a man!

Bear hunting was a passion. For the King Islanders of the Bering Sea, "polar bear hunting was very competitive, and some hunters, especially young ones, took great risks . . . to surpass the hunting success of their fellow hunters," the Jesuit missionary Bellarmine Lafortune observed in the 1930s. Knud Rasmussen in the 1920s asked an Inuk, "What is the greatest happiness in life?" The old hunter replied, "To run across fresh bear tracks and to be ahead of all other sledges." In 1967 when a group of Grise Fiord Inuit and I returned to Grise Fiord from a six-week, thousand-mile polar bear hunt, the people rushed down to meet us. The seven white pelts were spread on the snow for all to admire, and from our heavily laden sleds meat went to everyone in the village.

For much of that 1,000-mile trip I sat upon the polar bear pelt that covered our sled load. It was wonderfully soft and warm and at night, in our tent, we slept on it. To the Inuit the bear hunt was an affirmation of courage and maleness, but the bear was also food and magnificent fur. "February ninth [1938] . . . I saw a polar bear," the Inuk hunter Nuligak wrote in his memoirs. "I killed it; I was so happy thinking that the children would have something to eat, that I never forgot that day. I had killed a male white bear, big and fat."

In seal-rich springs when the hunting is good, polar bears who then eat nothing but blubber, blood and perhaps some entrails, can grow enormously fat. In 1984, scientists of the Canadian Wildlife Service tranquilized and tagged a male bear that weighed 1,800 pounds; he was swathed in a thick layer of blubber. James Lamont, a British sportsman who in 1859 shot walruses and polar bears near Spitsbergen, killed one "enormous old male bear . . . that produced nearly 400 lbs. of fat . . ." and a male bear killed by Fridtjof Nansen off East Greenland in 1883 ". . . gave altogether over thirty-eight gallons of oil." During our polar bear hunt, we, four Inuit and I and 29 sled dogs, ate an entire bear in three to four days. "The Greenlanders feed on the [bears'] flesh and fat; use the skins to sit on, and make of it boots, shoes, and gloves; and split the tendons into thread for sewing," Thomas Pennant wrote in his *Arctic Zoology* in 1784.

For the Inuit, polar bear fur had many uses. The Thule people of northwest Greenland make bear-skin overshoes to glide soundlessly across new-formed ice when they hunt seals in fall. Alaskan Inuit in the 19th century wore bear-skin knee protectors and one enormous, elbow-length mitten made of polar bear fur to hunt ringed seals in early summer upon water-soggy snow and ice. Like a bear, from whom their ancestors may have learned the technique, they crept up upon the resting seal, hiding behind the snow-colored fur mitten.

Polar bear fur is oily; neither water nor ice crystals adhere to it. When a bear comes out of the water, he shakes himself and an aureole of water droplets flies out of his fur. He rolls in dry snow that acts like a blotter and minutes later the bear is dry. When traveling by dog team, Inuit coat the sled runners with a film of ice so they glide nearly frictionless across the snow. A patch of polar bear fur is dipped in lukewarm water and pulled lightly across the runner to create this ice coating. When the Inuk is finished, he shakes the fur and it is dry. For reasons that I do not know, lice love the feel of polar bear hair. In former days, when Inuit were much troubled by lice, they used a special tool, a wooden stick two feet long with a claw-like ivory back scratcher at one end and a tuft of polar bear hair at the other. The stick was inserted beneath the clothes, lice clung to the polar bear hairs, were pulled out and eaten. "They eat me, I eat them," a Polar Inuk told Peter Freuchen.

The Polar Inuit of northwest Greenland are the last to hunt the great white bears with dogs (they have outlawed snowmobile hunting), and to these hunters the fur remains of immense importance, a symbol, warm and practical, of prowess and prestige. The men wear *nanut*, polar bear skin pants, perhaps the warmest, most durable, and, at current polar bear skin prices, among the most expensive pants in the world. Their wives' hip-high sealskin boots are trimmed with the silver-glistening mane fur of the male bear, and even the small sons of famous hunters wear polar bear trousers. Two or three men usually hunt together, and the bear's skin, fat and meat are divided according to ancient rules that are meticulously observed. The person who first spots the bear gets a major portion. Once in East Greenland, the Danish naturalist Alwin Pedersen related, a girl of 12 saw a bear far out on the ice. Her parents were away, so she ran and told a neighbor. He harnessed his dogs and pursued and killed the bear. "Before dusk, he had already delivered the skin and part of the meat to the little girl. . . ."

Elsewhere in the Arctic, polar bears are now hunted primarily for money. Good skins bring $1,000 to $2,000 (and were sold in the south for $3,000 to

"I have often noticed that to hunt and kill bear gives him a gratification . . . as great as that when he makes love to his wife."

—French scientist Jean Malaurie writing about the Polar Inuit, 1976

"Now that we have guns and skidoos, polar bears aren't dangerous at all. The thrill of the hunt is over."

—Ipeelie, Baffin Island Inuk talking to the American writer Richard C. Davids, 1970s

"To kill a bear can be considered neither as an exploit which enhances the status of the hunter nor as a sporting performance . . . there is too much brutality in it . . ."

—Alwin Pedersen, Danish naturalist who spent six years in East Greenland, 1930s

The hip-high sealskin boots of women and girls of the Polar Inuit in northwest Greenland are trimmed with the long mane fur of polar bears.

$5,000 in 1987). Men chase the bears with snowmobiles and this hunt is deadly efficient. The Canadian scientist George Wenzel accompanied Inuit from Resolute on Cornwallis Island on a polar bear hunt in 1979. They spotted a bear, a hunter raced after it with his fast machine until the animal, exhausted and overheated lay down. "The hunter . . . walked to within 10 m of the bear . . . fired once . . ." and the bear was dead. The men no longer need the meat and fat. As a rule, only the skin is taken and the gall bladder.

Throughout the ages, bears have been prized for different reasons. Ointment made from bear fat was used in many lands to ease the pain in rheumatic joints. (In ancient Rome bear fat was also used as axle grease.) To cure their colds, the Ainu make a soup of bear bones. And many Koreans believe so firmly that the gall bladders of bears, and especially those of polar bears, can heal stomach and liver ailments, that they pay more than $3,000 for each gall bladder. Given such monetary incentives, the polar bear hunt has inevitably become commercial. Canadian Inuit who can, under a quota system, kill 630 polar bears annually, hunt them primarily for the money they represent. Yet even now, a faint echo of the ancient reverence for the bear persists. The Inuit told George Wenzel that "the polar bear was fully as intelligent as a human being . . . [and warned him] never to joke about bears because to do so would bring future misfortune in polar bear hunting."

This reverence for bears was rarely shared by Europeans who came to the north. Most killed the bears for fun and profit, and some did so with an evil, casual cruelty. Favorite targets were females with cubs. Females were easy to kill since they never left their young and the cubs could be captured and sold to zoos. William Cass, surgeon aboard the whaler *Hercules* in 1831, described how for sport he and others chased a female bear and her two cubs in open water: "I fired at the old one but missed. They all swam close together; the mother appeared to caress the cubs with her nose. When we approached within 30 yards of them, the mother turned and charged open-mouthed. Candy, our harpooner, pushed the lance into her neck . . . [Finally] she dropped her head into the water, her last look being directed toward the cubs . . . who were swimming out to sea. We shot one of the cubs with a bullet. The other kept swimming around its brother. Milford threw a noose over the other's head and drew him up to the boat's bow, where he hung roaring and biting the boat's stem. He was strangled before reaching the ship."

Sealers followed the whalers to the northern ice. Dead seals made excellent bait; bears came from far and wide and were shot by the sealers or by paying sportsmen from the south who began to travel aboard sealing ships. Wintering trappers on Spitsbergen, who often used deadly set guns, killed hundreds of bears. The most famous of them, the Norwegian Henry Rudi, the "Bjørnekongen," the Bear King, killed about 800 polar bears in the 1920s and 1930s.

In 1952, sports hunting of polar bears near Spitsbergen began in earnest. Wealthy clients from Europe and America traveled at first on spruced-up seal-

"We travel from nowhere to nowhere in a world all white, suspended in time and space. Only the BEAR matters. It has become the center of our being."

—Fred Bruemmer, in diary kept during a six-week, 1,000-mile polar bear hunt with Ellesmere Island Inuit, 1967

ing ships and then on sleek luxurious yachts to the northern islands. The hunt was easy. The crew burned seal blubber to attract the bears, the hunter leaned over the side of the ship and shot the bear at point-blank range. The Norwegian Travel Service called it "one of the finest big game hunts in the world." In 1970, the sports hunters and a few trappers on Spitsbergen killed 515 bears.

In Alaska until 1950, only Inuit hunted polar bears, and they rarely took more than 120 a year. That year sports hunting began, and it soon gained worldwide notoriety because the bears were hunted with planes. The principal requisite for this hunt was money. For $3,000 at first, and soon for double and triple that sum, the hunter was assured a bear, for the method of hunting the bears gave them no hope for escape. Two planes took off together and flew far out over the pack ice in the Bering or Chukchi seas. When a bear was spotted, the hunter's plane landed and the other plane drove the bear to within easy shooting distance. Often both planes simply chased the bear until it collapsed. Then the sportsman landed and shot the bear. In 1965, the hunters killed about 300 bears, and 400 in 1966. "The polar bear is victim of a peculiar—and particularly repulsive—expression of man's egotism," noted the *New York Times* in a 1965 editorial. "Wealthy men have taken to hunting bears in Alaska from airplanes . . . This kind of hunt is about as sporting as machine-gunning a cow. Its only purpose is to obtain the bear's fur as a trophy for the floor or wall of someone's den."

Worldwide, the polar bear kill soared from about 600 a year in the 1950s to a high of 1,500 annually in the late 1960s. On September 6, 1965, delegates from the five circumpolar nations—Norway, Denmark (for Greenland), Canada, the United States and the Soviet Union—met in Alaska to discuss the fate of the polar bear. The most important question on the agenda was: "How many polar bears remain?" The Russians, who had given total protection to polar bears since 1956, claimed that in the entire north only 5,000 to 8,000 bears were left. Canadian scientists estimated that about 12,000 bears survived and the Americans thought about 19,000 bears still existed in the vastness of the Arctic. The truth was, no one knew. The polar bear's realm is immense: more than five million square miles of circumpolar land and frozen sea. Scientific research had been sketchy and knowledge of the polar bear was based largely on stories brought back by explorers and hunters.

Since then, the scientists have tranquilized and tagged more than 3,000 polar bears. Many have been equipped with radio collars. Thor Larsen, the Norwegian member of the five-nation Polar Bear Specialist Group, organized through the International Union for the Conservation of Nature and Natural Resources (IUCN), wrote in the magazine *International Wildlife* that "The newest bear collars transmit over the ARGOS satellite, and their signals are received and analyzed in Toulouse, France. All the participating biologists can link up to the Toulouse computer through ordinary telephone systems. From their offices the scientists can follow, and record, the migrations of polar bears

A bear recovering from the effects of a tranquilizing drug gets a friendly pat from a scientist.

Left: A tranquilized bear in a cargo net is weighed.

Right: Scientists from Canada and Norway take blood samples from a tranquilized bear for serological and genetic studies.

wandering around the Arctic thousands of miles to the north." Norway began to protect the bears in the Spitsbergen region and, said Larsen, "the bear population [there] has doubled from 1973 to 1983." He estimates the total polar bear population at 25,000. Ian Stirling of the Canadian Wildlife Service, this country's foremost polar bear expert, thinks they may now number more than 30,000.

The scientists of five nations caught the bears, counted the bears, tagged them, measured them, tattooed their lips, analyzed the milk of females and the caloric value of their main prey, the ringed seal. And slowly they pieced together the life history of the polar bear, this brand-new species, in evolutionary terms, that has become (after man) the superbly adapted master predator of the north.

Left: In a blinding blizzard bears scoop out shallow pits, often in the lee of a ridge, and sleep until the storm has blown itself out.

Right: Inuit polar bear hunters camp in a valley on Devon Island.

Above: Polar Inuit children in northwest Greenland romp on the ice while their father hunts. Their pants are made of polar bear skin, warm and extremely durable.

Left: The polar bear hunters use powerful telescopes to spot their prey.

Above: A Polar Inuk in northwest Greenland covers his cache of narwhal meat with heavy stones. Polar bears occasionally find and raid such meat caches.

Top right: A white whale killed but lost by Inuit has drifted ashore on an island, still linked to the plastic harpoon float, a feast for any bear that finds it.

Bottom right: Regal and unruffled, a polar bear caught in a steel cable snare awaits his scientist captors. The sand-filled drum acts as drag.

Opposite: An inquisitive bear and Len Smith, the designer of the Tundra Buggies used for bear watching.

Left: A scientist extracts a vestigial premolar from a tranquilized bear. Rings on the sectioned tooth tell the animal's age.

Above: A scientist tags a tranquilized polar bear.

OF BEARS AND SEALS

The polar bear was young and hungry. The ice covering the Northwest Passage, Lancaster Sound and Barrow Strait was disintegrating, ending the early summer seal hunt, and the bear had come ashore on the gaunt coast of Somerset Island. William Edward Parry of Britain's Royal Navy discovered this island on August 7, 1819, and said it was the most "barren and dreary" place he had ever seen, lunar plains and hills of frost-shattered, brownish limestone shards.

Yet there was life amid this seeming desolation and, guided by his superb sense of smell, the bear found some of it. "They smell farther than they see," Gerrit de Veer, chronicler of Barents's voyages, had already noted in 1594, and Alaskan Inuit have a saying that polar bears can smell a dead whale "from fifty miles away." The polar bear's hearing is also extremely acute. When John Kroeger and I lived on the tower at Cape Churchill and the bears were sleeping on the snow beneath, an arctic fox came by on silent furry feet and all our bears woke up. The biologist Ian Stirling watched a polar bear home in on a vole hidden in high grass. The bear listened intently to the minute chirp and whisper of the vole, pounced and got the little rodent.

The sense of vision, though, "appears to be poor in polar bears," says Stirling, who has spent thousands of hours observing them. The bears are probably myopic. They are also extremely curious. "The polar bear is an intelligent and crafty animal," wrote the explorer Fridtjof Nansen, "but it is cursed with intense curiosity." This may lead the bear to new sources of food. It can also bring him into conflict with humans who misconstrue the bear's intentions. Once, long ago, the bear specialist Charles Jonkel, then with the Canadian Wildlife Service, and I darted and tranquilized a young female bear near the shore of Hudson Bay. We weighed her, measured her, pulled a vestigial premolar which, sectioned, would tell us her exact age, tattooed her upper lip, glanced up from our work and there, a scant 15 feet away, next to Jonkel's gun and my cameras, sat a male bear observing us with the greatest interest.

The young bear I now watched on the shore of Somerset Island walked in a world that is nearly closed to us, the world of smells. Each breeze, each whiff of air brought him myriad scent messages, which his brain decoded and, if they promised food, guided his actions. He turned suddenly inland. An eider duck flew off her nest and he ate her large, olive-green eggs. Terns from a nearby colony rose in united fury and attacked the bear, white darts that came screaming out of the sky like Stukas and hit the bear's head with scarlet stiletto beaks.

Left: In early winter, the shore-bound bears are restless. They walk along the ice near shore, waiting for it to reach far out to sea, so they can hunt seals again.

Above: Polar bear on a tundra lake. Some bears sleep most of the summer and fall when they are ashore, however, a few roam far inland.

The circumpolar ranges of the polar bear and the ringed seal nearly overlap. Without this common seal, polar bears could not exist in the Arctic.

Annoyed, the bear shook his head. He found one tern nest and ate the eggs, then, bothered by the birds, he shuffled on. He examined every tidal pool. From one he pulled fronds of seaweed. He splashed into another with flailing paws trying to catch some arctic cod, finger-thick little fish. It seemed an enormous expenditure of energy for such a small reward. But these were only incidental snacks for a bear marooned on land. The polar bear's real realm is the ice and his vital food is seals.

Sometime in the latter part of the Pleistocene, about 250,000 years ago, some scientists believe, largely vegetarian, land-based brown bears of northernmost Siberia evolved into ice-based, seal-eating polar bears. Perhaps at first these bears found seal carrion along the coast and later ventured out upon the ice to hunt live seals. Although polar bears will eat anything from grasses to voles to whales, seals are the essence of their existence and where there are no seals polar bears cannot live. Over endless bear generations, they acquired a knowledge of seal behavior, and the principal stratagems of their hunt are based upon the weaknesses of their main prey, the small, numerous ringed seal (with a circumpolar population estimated by Stirling at between six and seven million animals), and the larger but much less abundant bearded seal.

In fall, as ice begins to cover the arctic seas and bays and inlets, each ringed seal cuts as many as ten to fifteen breathing holes into the ice with the long sharp claws of its foreflippers and, by repeated abrasion, keeps these cone-shaped holes open through ice that can become five to seven feet thick during the winter. In the murky world beneath the ice, the seal hunts arctic cod or crustaceans, finding its prey primarily by echolocation and by water turbulence picked up by its extremely sensitive vibrissae, long, droopy mystacial whiskers that pick up, like finely tuned antennae, vibrations in the sea. After diving from five to fifteen minutes, the seal surfaces in one of its holes, breathes deeply for ten to thirty seconds to reoxygenate its body and then dives again.

Warmly dressed in caribou parka, polar bear pants and sealskin boots, a Polar Inuk waits for a seal to surface in its breathing hole.

In late spring and early summer the seals haul out upon the ice beside their now much enlarged breathing holes, along leads (broad channels of open water), or, occasionally, at the floe edge, the limit of landfast ice. In favorite regions the seals may speckle the ice as far as the eye can see. "Floe rats," the whalers called them. A seal sleeps for a while, wakes up, looks carefully all around to make certain no danger is approaching, then, satisfied that all is safe, slumps into another brief nap. To hunt ringed seals successfully, said the explorer Vilhjalmur Stefansson, "all you have to know is one or two elementary facts about [their] habits and mental processes." Polar bears and Inuit are experts in seal psychology. Their survival and success in the Arctic is based upon this knowledge.

Polar bears are clever, versatile, opportunistic hunters. They know many ways of catching seals, but their main stratagems are "still-hunting," as Ian Stirling calls it (similar to the *aglu* hunting of the Inuit, whose ancestors, some scientists believe, may have adopted and adapted polar bear seal hunting techniques in order to survive in the Arctic), and "stalking," which is similar to *utoq* hunting, as the Polar Inuit of northwest Greenland call it.

The Inuk finds the seal's *aglu*, its breathing hole, with the help of trained dogs. He inserts an *idlak*, a long sliver of wood or bone, through the overlying snow into the breathing hole. As the seal surfaces to breathe, it pushes against the tip of the idlak and alerts the hunter above. When it moves he must strike. The hunter waits. It is −40° F. The arctic wind cuts like a knife. The hunter waits, motionless, like a statue, for the seal is life. "I have heard of a man who spent two and a half days at a breathing hole," Rasmussen tells. Ekalun of Bathurst Inlet, with whom I lived for seven months, once waited for many hours in bitter cold. Finally a seal surfaced in the aglu, the idlak jiggled, Ekalun drove his harpoon down in one smooth powerful motion—and missed. A chip of ice deflected his harpoon. "*Mamiena*," he said resignedly, "it is not good," and set out to find another aglu.

Polar bears are equally patient, although not always so philosophical about failure. (Masautsiaq, a Polar Inuit friend, saw a bear who had missed a seal by inches pound the ice in rage and frustration.) Guided by scent, the bear finds an aglu, scrapes the snow away and waits until the seal surfaces in this hole to breathe. It may be hours, it can be days, for the seal has many breathing holes. When the seal does come up in the aglu, the bear pins it against the ice wall with his sharp-clawed paw, grabs it nearly simultaneously with his teeth and yanks the seal upward through the constricted hole with such force that its bones buckle and break. It is a hunt at which mature bears excel. The young, too often, are impatient and abandon the vigil before the seal appears.

In the utoq hunt of spring and summer, some Inuit of eastern Canada and Greenland stalk the seals upon the ice hidden behind a large shield, now of canvas and formerly of white-bleached sealskin. Others, from Siberia to Greenland, approach the resting seal by pretending to be a seal. The hunter slithers across the snow while the seal sleeps. The instant it wakes, the hunter stops and makes seal-like movements that must be so perfect and convincing that the astigmatic seal regards him as a harmless fellow seal and, reassured, falls asleep again. To be successful in this hunt, "you have to think like a seal," an Inuk told me.

The bear, too, synchronizes his stalk with the sleep-wake rhythm of the basking seal. When the seal dozes, usually for 25 to 35 seconds, the bear advances "in a semi-crouched position, using whatever irregularities there were on the surface of the ice for cover," Stirling observed. The moment the seal wakes, the bear freezes, an indistinct, yellowish lump upon the ice. The seal raises its head, looks around for about four to five seconds and, if all seems well, goes to sleep again, and the bear resumes his cautious stalk. When he is within ten to thirty yards of the sleeping seal, the bear charges in a fantastic concentration of speed and power, a lethal blur of yellow across the ice. A stroke of the great paw, a bite at the back of the head that crushes the cranium and kills instantly, and the bear pulls the carcass away from the edge of the water. The death blow is always delivered with the left paw, say the Inuit, an opinion shared by their dogs who, according to the French scientist Jean Malaurie attack a bear "only from one side, for every good dog knows that bears are left-handed."

Although polar bears are not "snow white" (the usual color of their fur is a soft, lemon-colored wash, or the mellow yellow of old ivory), they blend well into the snow and ice landscape where they hunt. Only the large, coal-black nose stands out in stark contrast to the surrounding white and, said Stefansson, "it is unmistakable miles away." Some Inuit insist that stalking bears hide that

Harp seal surfacing in a lead among ice floes.

". . . in the capture of their prey, [polar bears] display a degree of instinct almost akin to reason . . ."

—Sir F. Leopold M'Clintock, RN, explorer, 1857

". . . five ringed seals were caught in the 602.7 bear hours of observation . . . or one kill per 5 bear days."

—Ian Stirling, polar bear specialist, Canadian Wildlife Service, 1974

"That seals often escape from the grasp of the bear is certain, for we [saw many bearded seals] . . . which were deeply gashed and scored by the claws of the bears."

—James Lamont, British sportsman, Spitsbergen, 1859

telltale nose behind a great white paw. (A trapped polar bear I once approached covered his face with a paw.) But Ian Stirling watched polar bears for hundreds of hours and not once did the cautious hunter use the forepaw "to cover the conspicuous black nose."

Most of the bear's hunts are not successful. During 602.7 hours of observation carried out by Stirling, the bears killed five ringed seals, "or one kill per five bear days . . . Four kills were made by still hunting and one by stalking . . ." Wary seals survive and these are usually older animals. Stirling and Eoin McEwan found that in Canada's Western Arctic "over 80% of all the ringed seals killed by polar bears were less than 2 years of age." An older seal, alarmed, dives instantly. A young seal, suddenly confronted by a bear or by an Inuk hunter, may hesitate a fatal second, staring in horrified disbelief. It is these young, incautious seals that are caught by young inexperienced bears who are learning to hunt. The cubs learn by watching their mother and later hunt apart from her, at first with little success because they are much too impatient. They creep too fast, the seal awakes, spots them and dives. They charge, impetuously, when they are still much too far from the seal, giving it ample time to escape. Sometimes, in play or in frustration, they prance across the ice, alarming all seals in the vicinity. Gradually, cubs and yearlings acquire the stealth and some of the patience of adult bears, and their first victims are nearly always young seals that slept too soundly and reacted too slowly.

Immediately after killing a seal, the bear begins to eat and he does so, noted Stirling, "in a very exacting manner . . . carefully using its incisors like delicate clippers to remove only the fat from the carcass, leaving the meat." Polar bears love blubber and, if hungry and given the chance, can devour vast quantities of it. One bear, killed near a whale carcass, had more than 100 pounds of blubber in his stomach. Studies carried out by Stirling and McEwan show that about 70 percent of the seal's total caloric value is in its fat. Much of the dead seal's blubber is converted to blubber upon the bear's body, an excellent insulation against cold air and the sapping chill of arctic water, and a vital energy reserve upon which the bear draws when hunting success is poor, or for those lean late-summer months that he must spend upon the food-poor land.

Polar bears are fastidiously clean, perhaps because fat and filth will mat their fur. The bears I watched at Cape Churchill washed after every meal. So did the bears Stirling observed in the high Arctic: ". . . a bear typically . . . stood in a pool of water . . . then licked off the upper and lower parts of the paws and its face, alternating between rinsing and licking. The washing procedure was repeated every 5 to 10 minutes . . ." Occasionally a bear returns repeatedly to his kill for additional meals. Usually, though, after having stripped the carcass of all or most of its blubber, licked up the blood and eaten some entrails, the bear wanders on, leaving the rest to less successful hunters—young bears to whom this may be vital food until they, too, become expert seal hunters—and to scavengers—arctic foxes, ravens and gulls.

Throughout winter and into spring, arctic foxes follow polar bears, as jackals follow lions, in hopes of leftovers. According to the Russian polar bear expert S.M. Uspensky, an arctic fox is very possessive about its polar bear. The first fox to attach itself to a bear tries to keep all other foxes away from its giant provider. The pushy little foxes irritate the bear. At Cape Churchill foxes boldly sneaked in to grab food. The bear hissed, lunged and struck with a mighty paw, but the little foxes nimbly skipped away and moments later, they were back pulling at the bear's food. Bear and fox travel far together. One fox, marked on Siberia's Taymyr Peninsula, crossed the entire Arctic Ocean and was caught in Alaska. Uspensky believes it followed the immense wanderings of a polar bear.

"Pihoqahiak," the ever-wandering-one, Inuit call the polar bear in the vivid imagery of their poems. It was once believed that polar bears roamed at random across the immensity of the Arctic, from continent to continent, eternal nomads of the north. Some do turn up in remote and unlikely places. In May, 1926, the explorers Lincoln Ellsworth and Roald Amundsen crossed the frozen Arctic Ocean in the airship *Norge* from Spitsbergen to Alaska. Near the "Ice Pole," (86° N, 157° W), "the most . . . inaccessible spot in the Arctic regions we saw one lone Polar bear track." In 1961, when I traversed the icecap of Spitsbergen with a British expedition, we came across polar bear tracks at the base of Newtontoppen, the highest mountain in the Spitsbergen Archipelago. Polar bears have been seen near the North Pole, an icy, hungry desert, which the Polar Inuit call *kingmersoariartorfigssuak*, "the place where one only eats (sled) dogs." Far to the south, at the latitude of Paris, France, and far inland, a female bear was shot in 1938 near Quebec's Lac Saint-Jean. Ice may have carried her into the Gulf of St. Lawrence and she may have tried to reach her arctic home by walking 600 miles overland. Japanese court annals as far back as the 7th century A.D. note that polar bears occasionally came ashore on Hokkaido. And a bear tagged in 1967 on Spitsbergen was shot a year later in southwest Greenland, more than 2,000 miles away.

Such bears with wanderlust are the exception. The recapture of tagged animals indicates that most polar bears belong to geographically discrete populations. The majority of the marked animals never wandered more than 100 miles from the place where they were captured. In Alaska "The same individual animals tend to return to the same general . . . area in late winter and early spring each year," noted Jack W. Lentfer, the polar bear specialist of the Alaska Department of Fish and Game. The bears know their home regions and take overland shortcuts from one sea area to another. One busy polar bear highway, between Bracebridge and Goodsir inlets of Bathurst Island in Canada's high Arctic, is now officially known as Polar Bear Pass. Another polar bear migration route crosses tiny Halvmånøya (Halfmoon Island) southeast of Spitsbergen. Norwegian trappers in the past killed as many as 145 bears there in one season.

Every fall the same bears (and the same scientists) return to Churchill and

"At the most . . . inaccessible spot in the Arctic regions [the Pole of Inaccessibility, 86° N, 157° W] we saw one lone Polar bear track."

—Lincoln Ellsworth, crossing the Arctic Ocean in the dirigible *Norge*, May, 1926

"Presumably the bear is able to wander across the whole of the Arctic Ocean even up to the Pole itself."

—Fridtjof Nansen, aboard his ship *Fram* in the Arctic Ocean, 1895

"Pihoqahiak"—the ever-wandering one.

—Poetic Inuit name for the polar bear

"Before [the seal] could make the slightest movement the bear brought his paw onto its head and killed it with a single stroke."

—Alwin Pedersen, Danish naturalist, East Greenland, 1930s

Cape Churchill. Bears I first met as youngsters, and met again year after year, are now quite elderly. Linda, the friendly female I once fed and petted, was three years old when Charles Jonkel caught her in a steel cable snare in 1966. She returned to Churchill every year, always friendly and affable, a devoted but relaxed mother to the cubs she produced regularly at two-year intervals. But Linda loved the easy life, gorged on garbage, became enormously fat and strayed too frequently into the town of Churchill. She was finally classified as a "nuisance bear," caught and, at the age of 24, sent to a zoo in the south, where she will never hunt seals again.

Whenever possible, polar bears like to still-hunt. This method produces the highest caloric return for the energy expended. Stalking requires much more energy. Most demanding is probably the summer hunt of ringed seals and bearded seals. Adult ringed seal weigh 120 to 200 pounds. Their realm is the fast ice of bays and inlets, and the unstable ice of pressure ridges and leads beyond. The bearded seal is a large and melancholy-looking seal with enormous droopy whiskers that curl like tendrils when they are dry. It can weigh more than 600 pounds and has a hide so tough, Inuit make from it the extremely durable soles of their sealskin boots. The bearded seal is a benthic feeder. Its long, extremely sensitive vibrissae help it to find its food—cockles and whelks, crabs, shrimps and holothurian worms and such bottom fishes as flounder and sculpin. Between dives to a depth of about 300 feet, it rests near its breathing hole or, more often, on ice pans that are its drifting home.

To reach bearded seals and ringed seals in summer, polar bears employ the "aquatic stalk," as Ian Stirling calls it. It is a method that requires planning, caution and concentration. The Danish naturalist Alwin Pedersen witnessed a typical summer ringed seal hunt off East Greenland. The bear spotted the seal

During the moult seals are lethargic and very itchy. Short flippers make scratching difficult.

on a far floe, studied its position long and carefully, lowered himself into the water with utmost caution, "and let himself sink until only his muzzle remained above the surface . . . He swam toward the seal with the tip of his nose making only a very slight ripple on the surface of the water. When he was ten yards from the ice-floe he lifted his head cautiously . . . and then dived. Suddenly the thin skin of ice which had formed round the floe shattered into pieces, and the head of the bear appeared exactly underneath the seal . . . Before it could make the slightest movement the bear brought its paw onto its head and killed it with a single stroke."

On June 7, 1978, at Winton Bay, Baffin Island, Thomas G. Smith, a seal and whale expert of Canada's Arctic Biological Station, watched as "a large bear attacked an adult bearded seal which was hauled up beside its hole on the fast ice. The bear entered the water through a hole in the ice about 400 meters from the seal and over a period of 32 minutes worked its way toward the bearded seal. [The bear swam beneath the ice] and was seen to come up to breathe at other seal holes twice during this time. When the bear got to the bearded seal hole the seal quickly dove down into the water and a great amount of splashing was seen." The large seal, though wounded, escaped and the bear hauled out on the ice. The bearded seal is a great catch, but even for the powerful polar bear a very hard one to hold. Often the seal twists away and slides into the saving sea. James Lamont, a British sportsman who hunted near Spitsbergen in 1859, found "That seals often escape from the grasp of the bear is certain for we [saw many bearded seals] . . . which were deeply gashed and scored by the claws of the bears." Five of six bearded seals collected by Smith at Winton Bay had "claw marks and bite marks on their bodies."

In March and April when polar bear mothers and cubs emerge from their winter dens, ringed seal pups are born in cleverly hidden subnivean lairs. Wherever snow is deep, near pressure ridges or large ice hummocks, ringed seal females cut aglus (holes) into the ice, then excavate oval lairs beneath the hard, compacted arctic snow that covers and shields their hiding places. Bears patrol pressure ridges methodically, and their acute sense of smell helps them to detect the seal's *nunarjak*, as Inuit call the birth lair.

The newborn pup is such a tiny morsel, the bear may not even eat it. What he hopes to catch is the female when she is in the lair with her pup. A female seal will not return to a den that seems in any way changed or damaged. So the bear, Tom Smith has found, uses a very clever ruse. He cautiously digs a hole into the seal's lair and sticks his head into it "thus preventing light penetration and giving the seal the impression of an undisturbed lair." When the seal surfaces in the aglu, unaware of the deadly danger, the bear grabs it and kills it. The bear's other method of killing seals in their lairs is quick and decisive. He smells from a long distance that a den is occupied and then, says Smith, "from a distance as far as 50 to 100 meters downwind, the bear will rush and jump on the lair often pinning and killing the occupant."

A cautious harbor seal comes ashore.

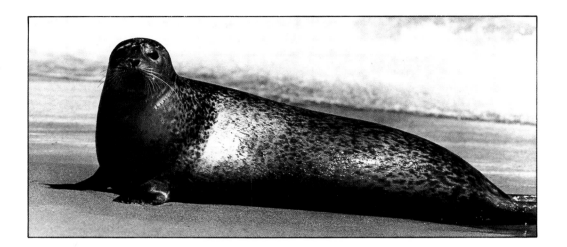

A group of harp seals in a lead. These seals are gregarious and often swim together in pods of from twenty to thirty animals.

Occasionally polar bears hunt bigger game, walruses and whales, but a one-ton walrus bull with huge ivory tusks is a formidable opponent and early accounts favor the walrus. "He is continually at war with the White Bear . . . and often kills him," wrote Hans Egede, the "Apostle of Greenland," in 1736, and Thomas Pennant in his *Arctic Zoology* of 1784, relying on the tales of explorers and whalers, stated that polar bears "are at constant enmity with the Walrus . . . the last, by reason of its vast tusks has generally the superiority . . . but frequently both combatants perish in the conflict." In water, the walrus can kill the polar bear. It swims faster than the bear. It dives, comes up beneath the bear and stabs him with its tusks. On ice, polar bears sometimes sneak up on a herd of resting walruses, charge suddenly to stampede them into the sea, grab a laggard calf and drag it away and kill it before its powerful mother can come to its rescue.

White whales sometimes become trapped by encroaching ice and as winter progresses their area of open water becomes smaller and smaller. When polar bears find such a *savssat*, they may have a prolonged feast, but most whales escape. In 1979, Inuit hunters with whom I traveled in Hudson Strait harpooned and killed a beluga. The animal had some time ago been attacked by a bear. Its sides and back were deeply grooved and lacerated and its melon, the fatty bulbous forepart of its head, had been torn off. The dreadful wounds had healed. The whale had escaped one arctic hunter only to fall prey to another.

When the ice, their hunting platform, melts, the bear must come ashore, and for most of them lean times begin. Some simply estivate. They dig shallow pits into sand dunes near shore, curl up and snooze away the food-poor months of summer and fall, living off their fat reserves. Once, on a polar bear survey with Charles Jonkel, I flew along the southern coast of Hudson Bay and dozens of bears popped out of their pits to stare at the passing plane.

Other bears wander along the coast hoping to find food. They hunt tiny lemmings and voles. They eat seaweed. They swim beneath moulting geese and pluck them down into the water. A bear near Churchill stalked goose decoys with patience and finesse, pounced, and when he only got a mouthful of papier-mâché, flattened in anger every decoy in sight. David Crantz, a Moravian missionary, in his classic work about the Greenland Inuit published in 1765, includes some notes on polar bears who in summer "live upon birds and their eggs." Bears raid eider colonies, kill all ducks who sit too tight on their nests and eat the eggs. Some years ago, I went with Ooloopie Killiktee of Lake Harbour on Baffin Island, and with his family, on a long trip to the Savage Islands to collect eider eggs. On a previous trip, he told me, a polar bear had discovered his cache of eggs for the summer and fall and had eaten more than 1,000, the equivalent of at least 2,000 chicken eggs.

When all else fails, polar bears, the largest carnivores on earth, will browse placidly in arctic meadows. The explorer John Davis killed three bears in 1585 near Cape Walsingham on Baffin Island and "found nothing in their mawes; but we judged by their dung that they fed upon grasse . . ." William Scoresby, the 19th-century English whaler-naturalist saw so many bears graze upon a lush meadow in East Greenland, they reminded him of "sheep on the common," and on Saint Matthew Island in the Bering Sea, American observers in 1874 saw about 250 polar bears "grazing and rooting about like hogs in a common."

The bears are only biding time. They patrol the coast impatiently, waiting for ice to cover the sea so that they can hunt seals again. On the day the ice is strong enough to hold their weight, the bears leave the land which offers them so little. Their true realm is the ice and the sea, that vast circumpolar region of the north, still rich in whales and seals and birds and bears, that Russian polar bear specialist S.M. Uspensky has called "the Arctic ring of life."

"We found nothing in their mawes; but we judged by their dung that they fed upon grasse . . ."

—John Davis, explorer, Baffin Island, 1585

A bear examines a seal's breathing hole. He will stand or lie near it for hours, sometimes for days, waiting for the seal to surface.

Left: According to an old Inuit tale, a polar bear stalking a seal hides his conspicuous black nose with his paw. A bear does occasionally cover his face with a huge paw.

Above: Foxes "adopt" bears and follow them all winter long eating scraps of food left by their massive providers.

Top left: Polar bears patrolling the arctic coast in summer often find eider ducks despite their superb camouflage. The brooding bird flies off at the last moment and the bear eats the eggs.

Bottom left: In summer when food ashore is scarce, polar bears sometimes catch lemmings, small fare for such giant hunters.

Right: Murre colony on Digges Island in Hudson Bay. Henry Hudson took birds from this cliff in 1610; Inuit hunt them and polar bears pick dead murres from the beach.

Bears live in a world of smells. Their superb sense of smell guides them to food.

Above: The bear's yellowish fur blends with the sere grass near the coast.

Overleaf: Bears patrol the beach near Cape Churchill.

Above: An arctic fox that did not watch is killed and eaten by a polar bear.

Top right: The bear pins whale carrion with his paw and rips off bite-sized pieces.

Bottom right: After licking his paws, a polar bear rubs on ice and snow to clean himself.

A polar bear licks his paws clean. If there is water near the kill, the bear will wash his paws from time to time.

Above: Hiding behind a white screen, an Inuk hunter takes aim at a ringed seal.

Top left: Herring gull in the late evening on the shore of a fiord in northern Labrador.

Bottom left: Harbor seals pup and moult on beaches. On rare occasions polar bears kill one of these coastal seals.

Right: Icebergs, calved from Greenland glaciers and shaped by water and wind, near the coast of northern Labrador.

Above: Nearly spread-eagled, a bear walks on very thin ice, ice too thin to support the weight of a man.

Right: Young bear mirrored in water-flooded ice.

MOTHERS AND CUBS

The bears assembled at Cape Churchill were hungry and irritable. Winter, with its promise of ice and fat seals, normally begins here in October. Now it was late November, there was as yet no ice on Hudson Bay and bears and bear watchers were still at the cape. None of us had ever seen so many bears. In the morning, 45 polar bears lay around our Tundra Buggy, 30 of them large males. Three were extremely old, including the age-blasted, fear-haunted King Lear, a once-great bear now near the end of his life. At night, some of the large bears reared up, leaned against the Tundra Buggy and rocked the ten-ton vehicle with such force, cups slid off the table. One night a bear ripped off part of the Tundra Buggy's sheet metal covering with a rapid-fire pop-pop-pop of pulled rivets. Then came the scrunching sound of yielding insulation, the inside paneling splintered and the beam of my flashlight showed a bear shoulder-high in our sleeping quarters. We hit him with a pan and he retreated, hissing and angry.

Seven people watched the polar bears in 1983 at Cape Churchill, one for the first time, all others had long ago succumbed to that atavistic fascination bears have for us, however diverse our backgrounds. There was Dan Guravich, World War II tank commander turned geneticist, and now a world-famous nature photographer; Len Smith, designer of the Tundra Buggies, a mechanical genius with a strange empathy for motors and for bears; Roy Bukowsky, a biologist turned businessman, who remained imprinted upon bears; Billy Mills, a brilliant Louisiana poet, who wrote of us that "We had come to behold the white lord," and who wrote of the bear, "Without me you walk in deserts. / Imprison me, you cage yourself"; Fred Treul, president of a brass-casting company, who combined an encyclopedic knowledge of metallurgy with an abiding love for bears and who returned to the cape each year; Anne Fadiman of LIFE magazine, petite and charming, a sparkling foil for Mills's rapier wit, who came to write about bears and men and, when one of the bears mauled one of the men wrote "A Tale of Arctic Beauty and Brutality"; and I, who had watched polar bears for half a lifetime, then dying of cardiomyopathy, watching the bears with the heightened sensibility of one knowing that he would probably never see them again.

One gloomy day a rare bird landed near the Tundra Buggy, an ivory gull from the highest Arctic. Excited, we forgot our usual caution. Fred Treul leaned far out of the window, supporting his heavy Hasselblad lens. A bear, one of the

Left: A bear family climbs an ice block near the sea to get a wider view.

Above: When any danger is near, the cub stays close to its massive mother.

starving ancient males, reared up silently beneath him and grabbed his arm. "A bear's got me!" Treul said in a shocked but quiet voice. In those vital, frozen seconds while all of us wondered what best to do, Bukowsky sprang to the window and with his bare fist struck the animal three times upon its extremely sensitive nose. The bear grunted, glared and let go. In those few seconds he had deeply punctured Treul's upper arm and ripped off most of the skin and flesh from elbow to wrist.

It was then the snowstorm started, the worst blizzard the Churchill region had known in years. With all hope of outside help gone, we drove blindly through a white world gone mad. The Tundra Buggy broke through the ice of a tundra lake. We all continued in a small tracked vehicle, Len Smith coaxing the utmost from a dying motor to save a dying man. That nightmare 50-mile journey through night and blizzard lasted 13 hours, yet Treul, the placid Milwaukee executive, though gray with pain, never complained. When we reached Churchill and he was bound by special plane for Winnipeg and expert medical care that saved his life and arm, he feebly waved us close and whispered, "Don't let them shoot the bear!"

Before that tragedy, we had watched a near-tragedy of a different kind. In summer when the ice breaks up on Hudson Bay, forcing the bears ashore, the males, as a rule, remain near the coast and females with cubs go inland. This season the ice was so late in forming, some females came to the cape, skirted the males, hopefully examined the sea and, disappointed, walked back inland, the roundish roly-poly cubs walking close to their mothers.

On November 23, there were 43 bears at the cape, 28 near the Tundra Buggy. A young female with two cubs approached. A crowd of bears attracts bears. It may mean food. It was hunger, no doubt, and inexperience that made her advance towards the massed males. She turned frequently to talk to her cubs in raspy, deep-throated grunts and the terrified tykes trotted obediently directly behind her. The males ignored her, but she appeared extremely tense and nervous. When she was 20 yards away, she charged the nearest male, roared, clawed and bit. He was more than twice her weight, but he roared back, recoiled and ran. She rushed back to her frightened cubs and immediately attacked the next male.

The roaring and commotion began to interest the bears. While their mother attacked with hysterical fury one male after another, none of whom had provoked her except by their presence, the cubs huddled together, desperately afraid. Now four large males converged upon them from different sides. The youngsters fled and the sight of running cubs excited the males. Three of them pursued the cubs, not really in earnest but at a leisurely trot. Their mother charged two more males (she routed six males in less than six minutes), the last with such impetuous fury that in fleeing he stumbled and fell. She turned and called her cubs. They were already far away. The three great males were gaining. The female called and galloped along the coast. Suddenly she heard the

Mother and cub rout a male bear.

frantic bawling of her cubs and raced after them. The three males immediately abandoned their half-hearted chase and the female led her cubs away.

Normally, male and female polar bears rarely meet except during mating time in April or in May. Since their ice realm is labile, polar bears have no fixed territories. They might meet nearly at random on the vastness of shifting ice. But a female in oestrus improves the odds by laying down a urine scent trail that usually assures her a throng of eager suitors. The males who played so amiably in fall, their movements as gentle and measured as a minuet, now fight rivals in dead earnest and kill them if they can. The seven Dutch whalers who spent the winter of 1633–34 on Spitsbergen may have witnessed such a battle when they saw "two bears fighting fiercely, clawing, biting and growling at each other for quite an hour and a-half . . . ."

Young males rarely enter these contests. It is the mature males, weighing 600 to 1,000 pounds and more, that face and attack each other. They stand and glare, then rush and bite and claw, rear up and rip the opponent's neck and chest and head. The weaker bear breaks and retreats, panting and bleeding. He turns and runs, and in a second the victor is upon him and rakes his rump with finger-long razor-sharp claws. The wounds look terrible but usually heal quickly. The Canadian biologist Malcolm Ramsay captured an adult male in March with a "suppurating wound" the size of a baseball mitten near his left ear and an "open wound on the right foreleg." When Ramsay caught the same bear eight months later "the wounds were completely healed and only minor scars were found." The victor, the strongest, heaviest, most determined male, follows the female for days and sometimes for weeks. They mate repeatedly and occasionally violently enough to snap the male's finger-thick baculum, his penis bone.

The fertilized egg divides, and divides again and again on the path to new life, and then suddenly ceases to develop. It remains dormant in the mother's womb, a minute speck of suspended life, until four to five months later, in September, when implantation, so long delayed, begins and embryonic growth resumes. During this time the female hunts assiduously to amass the fat reserves that, metabolized, will sustain her life and that of the coming cubs while she may have to fast for as long as eight months. "Polar bears may have adapted to survive longer fasts than any other mammal," Ramsay notes, and Dr. Ralph A. Nelson, formerly of the Mayo Clinic and now with the University of Illinois, wrote in admiration that "the adaptation of the bear in winter can best be described with one word, extraordinary."

In the 1770s, the famous Hudson's Bay Company trader and explorer Samuel Hearne, who lived for years at Churchill, shrewdly observed that although most bears go out onto the ice of Hudson Bay in winter to hunt seals, "the females that are pregnant seek shelter at the skirts of the woods, and dig themselves dens in the deepest drifts of snow they can find, where they remain in a state of inactivity, and without food, from the latter end of December or January, till the latter end of March; at which time they leave their dens, and bend their

"Never harass or antagonise a bear."

—From advice booklet published by the Manitoba Department of Mines, Natural Resources and Environment

"Polar bears are promiscuous and mating involves ferocious competition between males. . . ."

—D.R. Urquhart and R.E. Schweinsburg, Canadian polar bear specialists, 1984

course towards the sea with their cubs; which, in general, are two in number." The exact location of this major polar bear denning area was discovered by Charles Jonkel in the winter of 1969–70 in the forest and lake region south of Churchill.

The polar bear population of western Hudson Bay "appears to be unique in several ways," Ramsay and Stirling have noted. Since they are the southernmost polar bears in the world, they spend more time ashore than bears further north where the ice lasts longer. They are the most fecund of all polar bears. Studies carried out by Ramsay and Stirling show that they have "the highest natality rate, the highest mean litter size, and the shortest breeding intervals of any population of polar bears in the world." And some females of this southern polar bear population winter in earth dens, usually dug into the steep banks of lakes. Some dens, Ramsay found, are "relatively clustered. On one southeast-facing lakeshore more than 35 earthen dens were counted along 15 km of shoreline." I have crawled into many of these dens, after making absolutely certain no one was at home. A short tunnel leads to an oval chamber, dark, dank and cool in summer, filled with the earthy smell of roots and peaty soil. A few polar bears den even further south, on Akimiski Island in James Bay, at the latitude of Amsterdam and Dublin.

Pregnant females are drawn to the denning region where they were born, areas where snow conditions are nearly always ideal for excavating winter dens. These remote nurseries are dotted around the top of the globe: on Wrangel Island, off northeastern Siberia; on Franz Josef Land, north of Russia, only 600 miles from the North Pole; on Kong Karls Land in the Spitsbergen Archipelago; on Southampton Island in Hudson Bay; on the Simpson Peninsula on the Gulf of Boothia, in Canada's eastern mainland Arctic; along the northeast coast of Greenland. In this region, larger than Europe, much of it rarely seen by humans, all major denning areas are now probably known. Many minor ones remain to be discovered. In 1977, the Canadian biologist Ray Schweinsburg visited the remote Gateshead Island in Canada's M'Clintock Channel and found there nine polar bear dens. He returned in 1982, and this time discovered 15 dens on the island. A few bears den upon the frozen sea, as much as 100 miles from land. Jack Lentfer of the Alaska Department of Fish and Game has found such dens both "on fast and drifting ice." The snow dens are usually "on heavy, multi-year ice adjacent to old pressure ridges," solid ice, but nevertheless ice that is in constant movement. A pregnant female who went into her winter snow den upon the ice just north of Alaska's Barter Island, emerged five months later with her cubs 100 miles north-northwest of Point Barrow, having drifted slightly more than 400 miles.

Females tend to be solitary. Although they winter in the same general area, their dens are usually far from one another. But in a few places, perhaps because snow conditions are ideal, they "den in colonies," as Thor Larsen puts it. In 1980 he found 77 dens in one small area of Spitsbergen, "some only 60 feet

"Although expending about 4,000 kilocalories per day [for many months] . . . the bear neither eats [nor] drinks . . . the adaptation of the bear in winter can best be described with one word, extraordinary."

—Dr. Ralph A. Nelson, Mayo Clinic, 1980

apart." On Wrangel Island dens are clustered on the slopes of the Drem-Head Mountains, often less than 100 feet from each other. Two females denned so close to each other, only a two-foot-thick snow wall separated their winter quarters.

Nearly all denning sites are far from humans. Yet one den beneath a rock overhang on the north shore of Siberia's Chukotski Peninsula, occupied by female bears in three successive winters, was only 100 yards from a highway, and on Wrangel Island a female denned so close to a village school that in spring children and teachers could watch from the window as the bear mother and her cubs emerged from the den.

In October or November, the pregnant female seeks a suitable spot for her den, often on a south-facing slope where prevailing northerly winds have laid down a thick layer of snow. She starts by digging a tunnel. She sweeps away the loose snow with her paw, then cuts into the hard snow beneath and chunks of snow roll down the hill. As in an Inuit home of former days, the entrance tunnel slopes upward. Since warm air is lighter than cold air, none of it will escape from the den downward through the entrance. Some scientists believe that long ago proto-Inuit patterned the vital design of their winter homes upon those of the polar bear. The tunnel is usually five to seven feet long. At its end, the female excavates an oval chamber, typically eight to ten feet long, five to seven feet wide, and about five feet high. (Some dens are larger, and on rare occasions a female digs out multi-chambered winter quarters.) The den walls and floor are hard, compacted snow, deeply scored with claw marks. Snow debris from the den plugs the entrance tunnel. The female immures herself for four to five months.

Outside, wind and snow soon efface all traces of the den. Inside it's cozy. The myriad air cells in the snow make it an excellent insulator. The temperature within the den may be 40° F warmer than the temperature outside. (An igloo, too, is surprisingly warm. Just the body warmth of two people will keep the temperature inside an igloo above freezing, even when it's −10° F and blowing outside.) The female scrapes a small air vent into the den roof to let stale air escape. (In captivity, female polar bears seem capable of anticipating bad weather. Before it comes, they plug the vent with straw.)

The cubs are born in December or early January and since only four months have passed since implantation, and growth of the fetus began, they are tiny. (There is an ancient belief, older than Aristotle and Pliny, both of whom repeated it, that baby bears are born as doughy gobs of matter and are licked into proper bear-cub shape by their mother. "*Un ours mal léché*," a poorly licked bear, say the French of a coarse person.) The cubs that may grow into mighty half-ton males, are rat-sized at birth, weigh only one-and-a-half pounds and are blind and deaf. Sparse fuzzy wool covers their pink bodies, except the nose and the rosy pads of their paws. Clinging with sharp sickle-shaped claws to the fur of their mighty mother, the cubs creep towards her chest and begin to suckle her fat-rich milk. (The milk I tried—from a tranquilized she-bear—had the consistency of thick cream and tasted strongly of cod-liver oil.) The milk contains 31 percent butterfat and 12 percent protein and is surpassed in nutritional value only by the milk of seals and whales. The cubs snuggle into their mother's deep-pile fur. She cradles them with her huge paws and breathes over them to keep them warm.

Most female polar bears mate at the age of four or five and some have cubs until they are 25 years old. (Some polar bears live long. In 1980, Dennis Andriashek, Ian Stirling's long-time assistant, tagged a bear on Canada's Devon Island that was 33 years old. In the mid-19th century a polar bear lived for 36 years at London's Regent's Park Zoo, and in this century a bear at the Chester, England, zoo lived to be 41 years old.) In all regions of the north, except western Hudson Bay, females usually have cubs at three-year intervals. About 40 percent of all west Hudson Bay females leave their young when they are only one and a half years old (instead of a hefty two and a half years, further north) and have cubs every second year. These bears also have the largest litters. Most females have twins. Very young mothers, and very old ones, often only have a single cub. About one percent of all polar bears has triplets, except those fertile bears of western Hudson Bay. There, Ramsay found, "triplets made up 12% of the cub-of-the-year litters observed in spring . . . and even one quadruplet litter was captured."

The cubs nurse frequently and grow quickly. When they are cold, they whimper and their mother hugs them closer. When they are 26 days old, they begin to hear; at 33 days their eyes open. Their sparse, silky natal fur becomes longer, coarser and denser. When they are two months old, the cubs weigh 12 to 15 pounds and they begin to explore their dark domain. They play and romp and sometimes one can hear them squeal. Their mother is sleepy and indulgent. She reclines against the den wall and dozes, expending as little energy as possible. But if any danger threatens, she is immediately wide awake. The Canadian scientist Richard Harington once opened the roof of a den on Southampton Island in Hudson Bay. "A glistening black eye and twitching muzzle were instantly applied to the aperture by the mother bear. While she paced the den floor beneath us, uttering peevish grunts, we were just able to discern her two young cubs huddled against the far wall of their snow house."

Normally the months pass quietly. While the storms of winter rage outside, the bear family lives comfortably in its snug lair deep within the snow. The female keeps the den very clean. When the floor becomes soiled with the cubs' urine and feces, she covers it with a layer of fresh snow scraped from the ceiling. (During all these months, the female does not eat or drink, neither does she urinate or defecate.)

Usually in March, the female digs out a tunnel and the cubs emerge from their cramped and gloomy den into the dazzling, infinite world of the Arctic. The cubs are now densely furred, weigh 20 to 25 pounds and are fox terrier-sized but chubbier. They are curious and playful. They have suddenly come into a fascinating new world, a world full of new smells and sights and sounds. They rush and play and explore. When they go too far away, the female growls and they obediently run back to her. The female remains in the vicinity of the den for five to ten days. She scrapes away the snow and eats some of the plants, mosses and wilted sedges, or the sourish, watery crowberries that keep well during the winter.

The cubs are round-buttocked and round-bellied and full of the enchantment of life, of freedom and of space. Watched by an indulgent but observant mother, they prance and frolic in the snow. The favorite game is to schuss down the snow slopes on their bellies, hindpaws and frontpaws outstretched. The Danish naturalist Alwin Pedersen watched them on East Greenland. The cubs were glissading down a snow slope, a game "which they obviously enjoy . . . The mother stood down at the bottom of the slope, catching the infant gambollers with her front paws each time they arrived at the bottom, happily growling and completely covered with snow." The cubs love the game. It also strengthens them and gives them the agility and stamina for their march to the sea and the long wanderings they will make with their mother as she searches the ice for seals.

Most dens are five to ten miles from the sea and the female leads her cubs on a straight course set with great precision. Ramsay tracked 64 polar bear families for 577 miles during his five-year study and found that "a striking feature of the family group tracks were their linear nature over intervals of 5 km or longer."

Bear family at the edge of the frozen sea.

From time to time the female stops, scoops out a shallow pit, reclines and lets her weary little wanderers nurse. In the region west of Hudson Bay where polar bears travel through forest to reach the sea, the snow can be soft and deep. Normally the cubs follow in the tracks made by their mother. But in an emergency, they ride upon their mother's back. Dan Guravich saw females fleeing from a helicopter plow through deep snow at a steady trot, their cubs clinging to their backs "like frightened little jockeys." (One summer I traveled by canoe on a bay of northern Baffin Island with scientists who were studying narwhal and we met a bear family crossing the bay. The mother swam strongly for the opposite shore, dog-paddling with her great front paws and trailing her hind legs. The two chubby cubs, about eight months old, rode piggyback, their sharp-clawed paws dug into their mother's thick fur. When they slipped, the female dived and surfaced beneath them, giving the cubs a chance to get a more secure grip.)

Usually the trip to the sea, though tiring, is without danger. On rare occasions, wolves may attack the family. Ramsay and Stirling describe such a case, a story told by tracks in the snow. The family, a female with two cubs, was halfway to the sea when it was intercepted by two wolves. While one wolf harried the mother, the other ran at the cubs, grabbed one and carried it away. The mother chased the wolf, then raced back to her remaining cub just before the other wolf reached it. The female led the surviving cub away and "the wolves did not follow. The dead cub was completely eaten; only bits of fur and blood remained."

The female has fasted for five to eight months. She has given birth and reared two cubs. Now her fat reserves are nearly depleted and she urgently needs food. March, fortunately, is the month of abundance, the month ringed seals have their pups in lairs beneath the snow. One day in early April I followed the tracks of a polar bear family on Jones Sound in Canada's far north. It was one of those glorious days when the Arctic is perfection: the sky a deep robin's egg blue shading to cool green near the horizon, the snow brilliantly aglitter, the air as clear and cool as chilled champagne. The female bear walked downwind from a pressure ridge, stopping frequently, testing the air, searching for *nunarjaks*, the seals' birth lairs. She found a lair and smashed its roof. Two limp, furry flippers in the snow were all that remained of the seal pup, a tiny meal for a hungry bear. While the mother patrolled methodically, her cubs played. They raced up inclined sheets of pressure ice, then slid and tumbled down. They romped in the snow, then, called, galloped to catch up with their mother. At the third lair the bear killed both the seal and its pup. Her huge tracks and the small tracks of her cubs showed they had eaten together.

The mother nurses the cubs for at least a year, but the cubs also share her meals. They watch her hunt and they begin to hunt themselves. At first their efforts are partly play. Stirling watched a polar bear family in the high Arctic and "on several occasions cubs sprinted across the ice and dove into the water

The mother swam behind her cub "shielding it from danger and urging it along. She continued to do this even after a ball had shattered her spine. . . ."

—Edward W. Nelson, ethnologist, Alaska, 1887

head-first in a manner similiar to the final rush of an adult bear for a seal at the end of a stalk." When cubs stalk a seal, they soon spook it for they are far too impatient and move too quickly. They then run idly about on the ice, often spoiling their mother's hunt. But the cubs learn fast. Towards the end of the summer they may occasionally succeed in catching a sleepy young seal. (Animal trainers consider polar bears highly intelligent and the animals learn quickly. Early in this century, the German animal trainer Willy Hagenbeck had a stunning circus act with 70 polar bears in a mammoth cage. The explorer Roald Amundsen saw it, was impressed and asked whether Hagenbeck could train polar bears to pull a large sled. In nine weeks 21 bears were trained and ready to work in the north as a bear team, but neither Hagenbeck nor their keeper, Reuben Castang, were willing to go on polar expeditions and the idea was finally dropped.)

At the time of Hagenbeck, there was a plethora of captive polar bears in Europe. Sealers, whalers and walrus hunters shot female bears and brought back their cubs. Explorers returned with cubs. Sports hunters killed all the bears they saw and took home cubs. All planned to sell the cubs to zoos, menageries and circuses and already by the mid-19th century the bear cub market had been saturated.

It was easy to get the cubs. Thomas Pennant had noted in 1784 that "great is the affection between parent and young; they will sooner die than desert one another," and the explorer Fridtjof Nansen wrote in 1883, "She shows the greatest tenderness for them, and never leaves them even in the utmost danger." Hindered by the slow-moving cubs, the female was easy to shoot. Then, wrote Nansen, "I knew of an instance where the two small cubs, with signs of the greatest affection, followed the body of their mother, which had been shot, to the boat, jumped in after it, sat themselves down on it, and quietly let themselves be taken on board."

To acquire cubs was easy. To dispose of them could be more difficult. The British sportsman James Lamont shot a female in 1859 on Spitsbergen, brought home her cubs and then wrote to "nearly every wild-beast-keeper and secretary of Zoological Gardens in the United Kingdom, but as usual the 'British market was quite overstocked.' There was a 'glut' of bears in fact." He toyed with the idea of turning the bear cubs loose on his estate and inviting friends and neighbors for a battue. He dropped the idea because his beaters objected and eventually sold the cubs to the Jardin des Plantes in Paris, where the poor animals were "confined in one of the warm, dry dens used for the tropical Carnivorae."

In July in Hudson Bay and usually in August further north, the ice breaks up and melts and the bears must come ashore. In the south, some rest in shallow earth dens. In the far north, some dig snow beds or even dens on leeward slopes and doze away the days. When Ray Schweinsburg made a survey of northern Baffin Island, some bears were in summer dens and "numerous other bears loafed or lay on the lower beaches and coastal plains." One female and her cub had walked 35 miles inland. A few bears hunt, even very humble game. The explorer Sir Leopold M'Clintock tells of Captain Sherard Osborn who watched a female and two cubs catch lemmings, "the mother diligently turning over loose rocks . . . and the cubs watching the opportunity . . ." to rush in and grab the little rodents. After this hunt, the female reclined to let her cubs nurse and "Osborn shot the whole of this interesting family."

In late July or August, those females who have mated in spring and whose cubs are now two and a half years old, leave them, for soon they will return to their denning areas to raise a new generation. About 40 percent of the west Hudson Bay females leave their cubs when they are only one and a half years old. The hunting on Hudson Bay is presumably easier than in the far north and these youngsters have a good chance to survive.

At Cape Churchill these recently abandoned yearlings are alternately cheeky and pathetic. Until recently they walked in the shadow of an all-loving, all-mighty mother. They only had to cry for help, the plaintive call of a frightened cub, and the mother rushed to their defence. Now, alone and motherless among this horde of huge males, who could easily kill them if they could catch them (yearlings run much faster than large males), they must at times feel like Daniel in the lions' den. But there is a sort of "live and let live" etiquette among the massed bears at the cape (perhaps none of them want to get hurt before the hunting season starts), and in all the years I've watched the bears I have never seen a small bear injured by a great male. But I have seen a little 180-pound bear stand over a chunk of food and refuse to budge as a 1,000-pound male approaches. The small bear becomes as bristly as a frightened hedgehog, its head is low, its back is curved, and it growls and hisses savagely. The great bear oozes in. He probably could swat the little guy out of existence, but he nearly always uses the soft approach. They either eat together or, more often, the small bear finally loses his nerve and flees. All bears at the cape walk with the slow deliberation that is so typical for polar bears. Only the yearlings run—and have reason to run.

The bears are impatient. They are the bears of the ice, and as yet there is little ice. After a still, cold night, the bears test the thin layer of new ice in a cove. Nearly spread-eagled, a 1,000-pound male slides on huge furry paws across a film of ice so thin, it would not carry a human. The waves, greasy and gray with frazil ice, roll heavily against the coast and glaze the rocks and pebbles. Slob ice and pans drift in from the bay and congeal with the frazil ice and the new-formed *nilas*, the new ice. The nights are now extremely cold. Ice-pale auroras flow across the sky.

One morning the ice is finally strong enough and the bears can leave the land. The great males go first. Bears that have become friends leave in pairs. The yearlings leave; soon they are only yellow dots upon the vastness of the ice. At last, as if responding to a call, the females come with their cubs, and they too head out onto the fields of ice that are the true realm of the polar bear.

Mother and cub cross the sun-colored ice of a lagoon.

At the time of weaning, cubs are nearly as big but not nearly as heavy as their mother.

Cubs are playful; polar bear females are protective but indulgent mothers.

Above: A female and her cubs follow the shore in late fall, hoping to find food.

Right: A bleak winter day near the treeline. Polar bears den in this region, west of Hudson Bay.

The cub follows its mother like an obedient little shadow.

A chubby cub, its fur honey-yellow in the evening light.

Above: Cubs are born in a snow den in December or January. The family leaves the den in March and goes to the sea ice to hunt seals.

Right: A one-and-a-half year old cub, recently abandoned by its mother. Only on Hudson Bay where hunting is easy do female polar bears abandon their cubs at such a young age.

The outstretched front paw is often used as a pillow.

BIBLIOGRAPHY

Balikci, Asen. *The Netsilik Eskimo.* New York: Natural History Press, 1970.

Biggar, H.P. *The Voyages of the Cabots and of the Corte-Reals to North America and Greenland 1497–1503.* Tome X. Paris: Revue Hispanique, 1903.

——*The Voyages of Jacques Cartier.* Ottawa: King's Printer, 1924.

Biggar, H.P., ed. *The Works of Samuel de Champlain.* Toronto: The Champlain Society, 1933.

Boas, Franz. "The Central Eskimo." Sixth Annual Report of the Bureau of Ethnology, 1888. Reprint. Lincoln, Nebraska: University of Nebraska Press, 1964.

Bodfish, Hartson, H. *Chasing the Bowhead.* Cambridge: Harvard University Press, 1936.

Bruemmer, Fred. *The Long Hunt.* Toronto: The Ryerson Press, 1969.

——*Encounters with Arctic Animals.* Toronto: McGraw-Hill Ryerson, 1972.

——*Arctic Animals.* Toronto: McClelland and Stewart, 1986.

Campbell, Joseph. *The Masks of God: Primitive Mythology.* London: Viking Press, 1959. Reprint. Penguin Books, 1976.

Chernetsov, V.N., and Moszynska, W. *Prehistory of Western Siberia.* Montreal: McGill-Queen's University Press, 1974.

Conway, Martin W. *Early Dutch and English Voyages to Spitsbergen in the Seventeenth Century.* London: Hakluyt Society, 1904.

Crantz, David. *The History of Greenland.* London: Printed for Moravian Mission, 1767.

Davids, Richard C., and Guravich, Dan. *Lords of the Arctic.* New York: Macmillan Publishing Co., 1982.

De La Peyrère, I. *Relation du Groenland.* 1663. Reprint. London: Hakluyt Society, 1855.

DeMaster, Douglas P., and Stirling, Ian. "Ursus Maritimus." *Mammalian Species* (1981), 145: 1–7.

Dembeck, Hermann. *Animals and Men.* New York: Natural History Press, 1965.

Egede, Hans. *A Description of Greenland.* London: T. and J. Allman, 1818.

Freeman, Milton M.R. "Polar Bear Predation on Beluga in the Canadian Arctic." *Arctic* 26 (1973).

Freuchen, Peter. *Vagrant Viking.* New York: Julian Messner, 1953.

——*Ice Floes and Flaming Water.* New York: Julian Messner, 1954.

Freuchen, Peter, and Salomonsen, Finn. *The Arctic Year.* New York: Putnam, 1958.

Gad, Finn. *The History of Greenland.* 2 vols. Montreal: McGill-Queen's University Press, 1971.

Gosling, W.G. *Labrador.* London: Alston Rivers, 1910.

Hakluyt, Richard. *Voyages.* 8 vols. London: J.M. Dent and Sons, 1962.

Hall, Charles Francis. *Life with the Esquimaux.* 1864. Reprint. Rutland: Charles E. Tuttle Co., 1970.

Harington, C.R. "Polar Bears And Their Present Status." *Canadian Audubon Magazine,* January–February, 1964.

Hearne, Samuel. *A Journey from Prince of Wales' Fort in Hudson Bay to the Northern Ocean in the Years 1769, 1770, 1771, 1772.* Edited by Richard Glover. Toronto: The Macmillan Company, 1958.

Howell, F. Clark. *Early Man.* New York: Time-Life Books, 1971.

Ingstad, Helge. *Land under the Pole Star.* New York: St. Martin's Press, 1966.

Jones, Gwyn. *The Norse Atlantic Saga.* Oxford: Oxford University Press, 1986.

Jonkel, C.E. et al. *The Productivity of Polar Bears (Ursus maritimus) in the South-eastern Baffin Island Area, Northwest Territories.* Canadian Wildlife Service Prog. Notes 91 (1978).

Kane, Elisha Kent. *Arctic Explorations: The Second Grinnell Expedition in Search of Sir John Franklin 1853, '54, '55.* Philadelphia: 1857.

Kiliaan, H.P.L. "The Possible Use of Tools by Polar Bears to Obtain Their Food." *Norsk Polarinstitutt Arbok,* 1972.

Kirk, Ruth. *Snow.* New York: William Morrow and Company, 1978.

Koch, Thomas J. *The Year of the Polar Bear.* New York: The Bobbs-Merril Co., 1975.

Lamont, James. *Seasons with the Sea-Horses.* London: Hurst and Blacket, 1861.

Larsen, Thor. *The World of the Polar Bear.* London: Hamlyn, 1978.

——"We've Saved the Ice Bear." *International Wildlife,* July–August, 1984.

Larson, L.M., trans. *The King's Mirror.* New York: The American-Scandinavian Foundation, 1917.

Lentfer, Jack W. *Polar Bear Reproductive Biology and Denning.* Juneau, Alaska: Alaska Department of Fish and Game, 1976.

Lopez, Barry. *Arctic Dreams.* New York: Charles Scribner's Sons, 1986.

Lyall, Ernie. *An Arctic Man.* Edmonton: Hurtig Publishers, 1979.

Magnus, Olaus. *Histoire Des Pays Septentionavs.* Antwerp: Christophle Plantin, 1561.

Malaurie, Jean. *The Last Kings of Thule.* New York: E.P. Dutton, 1982.

Martens, F. *Voyage Into Spitzbergen and Greenland.* (in 1671) London: Hakluyt Society, 1855.

M'Clintock, F. Leopold. *The Voyage of the Fox in the Arctic Seas in Search of Franklin and His Companions.* London: John Murray, 1875.

M'Clure, R. *The Discovery of the Northwest Passage*. 1856. Reprint. Edmonton: M.G. Hurtig Ltd., 1969.

Mills, William. *Bears and Men*. Chapel Hill, NC: Algonquin Books of Chapel Hill, 1986.

Nansen, Fridtjof. *In Northern Mists*. London: William Heinemann, 1911.

Nelson, Edward W. "The Eskimo About Bering Strait." Eighteenth Annual Report of the Bureau of American Ethnology. 1896–1897. Reprint. Washington, D.C.: Smithsonian Institution Press, 1983.

Nelson, Richard K. *Hunters of the Northern Ice*. Chicago: University of Chicago Press, 1969.

Nero, Robert. *The Great White Bears*. Winnipeg: Manitoba Department of Mines, Resources and Environmental Management, 1971.

Nuligak. *I, Nuligak*. Edited by Maurice Metayer. New York: Pocket Book, 1971.

Nyholm, Erik S. "On Polar Bear Behavior in Spitzbergen." *Norwegian Polar Yearbook 1975–76*.

Oleson, T.J. "Polar Bears in the Middle Ages." *The Canadian Historical Review*, March, 1950.

Pedersen, A. *Der Eisbaer: Verbreitung und Lebensweise*. Copenhagen: E. Bruun and Co., 1945.

——*Polar Animals*. New York: Taplinger Publishing Co., 1966.

Pennant, Thomas. *Arctic Zoology*. (2 vol.). London: Robert Faulder, 1784.

Perry, Richard. *The World of the Polar Bear*. Seattle: University of Washington Press, 1966.

Ramsay, M.A., and Andriashek, D.S. "Long Distance Route Orientation of Female Polar Bears In Spring." *J. Zool., London* (A) 208 (1986): 63–72.

Ramsay, Malcolm A., and Stirling, Ian. "Interactions of Wolves and Polar Bears in Northern Manitoba." *Journal of Mammalogy*, November, 1984.

Ramsay, Malcolm A. "The Reproductive Biology of the Polar Bear: A Large, Solitary Carnivorous Mammal." PhD thesis, University of Alberta, Edmonton, Alberta, 1986.

Rasmussen, Knud. *Report of the Fifth Thule Expedition, 1921–1924*. Copenhagen: Gyldendalske Boghandel, Nordisk Forlag, 1930.

Renner, Louis L., S.J. *Pioneer Missionary to the Bering Strait Eskimos: Bellarmine Lafortune, S.J.* Portland, Oregon: Binford & Mort, 1979.

Rink, Henry. *Tales and Traditions of the Eskimo*. Edinburgh: William Blackwood and Sons, 1875.

Russell, Andy, ed. *Great Bear Adventures*. Toronto: Key Porter Books, 1987.

Russell, R.H. "The Food Habits of Polar Bears of James Bay and Southwest Hudson Bay in Summer and Autumn." *Arctic* 28 (1975).

Schweinsburg, R.E. "Summer Snow Dens Used by Polar Bears in the Canadian High Arctic." *Arctic* 32 (1979).

Schweinsburg, R.E. et al. "Distribution, Movement and Abundance of Polar Bears in Lancaster Sound, Northwest Territories." *Arctic* 35: 159–169.

Scoresby, William Jr. *Journal of a Voyage to the Northern Whale Fishery*. Edinburgh: Archibald Constable and Co., 1823.

Shimkin, E. "The Upper Paleolithic in North Central Eurasia: evidence and problems." In *Views from the Past*, edited by L.G. Freeman. The Hague: Mouton, 1978.

Smith, Thomas G. "Polar Bear Predation of Ringed and Bearded Seals in the Land-Fast Sea Ice Habitat." *Canadian Journal of Zoology* 58 (1980): 2201–2209.

——"Polar Bears, Ursus maritimus, as Predators of Belugas, Delphinapterus leucas." *Canadian Field Naturalist* 99 (1985): 71–75.

Soergel, W. *Die Massenvorkommen des Hoehlenbaeren*. Jena: Gustav Fischer, 1940.

Stefansson, Vilhjalmur. *My Life with the Eskimo*. New York: Collier Books, 1966.

Stirling, Ian. "Midsummer Observations on the Behavior of Wild Polar Bears." *Canadian Journal of Zoology* 52 (1974): 1191–1198.

Stirling, Ian and Eoin H. McEwan. "The Caloric Value Of Whole Ringed Seals in Relation to Polar Bear Ecology and Hunting Behavior." *Canadian Journal of Zoology* 53 (1975): 1021–1027.

Stirling, Ian et al. "The Ecology of the Polar Bear Along the Western Coast of Hudson Bay." Occasional Paper 33. Ottawa: Canadian Wildlife Services, 1977.

——"Population Ecology of the Polar Bear Along the Proposed Arctic Islands Gas Pipeline Route." Edmonton, Alberta: Canadian Wildlife Service, 1978.

Stirling, Ian; Calvert, Wendy, and Andriashek, Dennis, "Polar Bear Ecology and Environmental Considerations in the Canadian High Arctic." In *Northern Ecology and Resource Management*, edited by Rod Olson. Edmonton: The University of Alberta Press, 1984.

Struzik, Ed. "Nanook." *Equinox* 1, January–February, 1987.

Taylor, Mitchell; Larsen, Thor; and Schweinsburg, R.E. "Observations of Intraspecific Aggression and Cannibalism in Polar Bears. (Ursus maritimus)." *Arctic* 38 (1985): 303–309.

Taylor, William E. and Swinton, George. "Prehistoric Dorset Art." *The Beaver*, Autumn, 1967.

Uspenski, S.M. *Der Eisbaer*. Wittenberg Lutherstadt: A. Ziemsen Verlag, 1979.

Urquhart, D.R. and Schweinsburg, R.E. *Polar Bear*. Yellowknife, NWT: Government of the Northwest Territories, Department of Renewable Resources, 1984.

Veer, Gerrit de. *A True Description of Three Voyages by the North-East Towards Cathay and China*. London: Hakluyt Society, 1853.

Vibe, Christian. *Arctic Animals in Relation to Climatic Fluctuations*. Copenhagen: C.A. Reitzels Forlag, 1967.

——"Thule-Eskimoernes Isbjørnejagter," *Grønland*, the magazine of *Det Grønlandske Selskap*, June, 1968.

Wenzel, George. "Inuit and Polar Bears: Cultural Observations from a Hunt near Resolute Bay, NWT." *Arctic*, 36: 90–94.